AF227625

Fr. Josiah Trenham

ENDURING LOVE

Laying Christian Foundations for Marriage

Patristic Nectar Publications is pleased to present this new pre-marital counseling theological workbook entitled Enduring Love: Laying Christian Foundations for Marriage. Marriage preparation, together with the sacred institution of marriage itself, has fallen on hard times in the culture of the post-Christian West. It is more important than ever for couples to saturate their hearts and minds with the glorious vision of holy matrimony presented by the Church in Holy Tradition and lived by countless married saints for the last two-thousands years. Here in the pages of Enduring Love couples will find inspired teaching from the Holy Scriptures, the writings of the Holy Fathers, and the service texts of the sacrament itself, on how to live in a genuinely Christian marriage in which the home becomes a domestic church. Each of the ten chapters contains both a succinct theological teaching and a workbook section with questions for the couple to work through together in preparation for marriage. Through Enduring Love may God inspire the hearts of those preparing to be married, and also those already married who would like to deepen their union and render it more pleasing to God and to themselves.

Enduring Love is dedicated to my faithful parishioners, the members of St. Andrew Orthodox Church - Riverside, California, who attended the lectures which became this book, and who helped fashion the study questions and exercises found at the end of each chapter. God grant you all many years!

Book layout and cover design by Andrew Ritchey, the Orthodox Design Company
www.orthodoxdesigncompany.com

Photos by Nick Mueller Photography
www.nickmuellermedia.com

ISBN 978-1-7350116-5-3

Patristic Nectar Publications
www.patristicnectar.org
info@patristicnectar.org

Table of Contents

Foreword

"Receive their crowns into thy Kingdom, preserving them spotless, blameless, and without reproach, unto ages of ages."

In his great poetic work On Virtue, St Gregory the Theologian (329-390) wrote:

> Who, then, has reunited in one what was separated, but marriage? And there is yet more: We are one another's hand, ear, foot, By the blessing of marriage that redoubles our strength, rejoicing our friends, desolating our enemies. Common joys are still happier and accord makes riches more precious, nay, it is more precious than riches for those who do not possess them. Marriage is the key of moderation of the desires, The seal of unbreakable friendship, ... The unique drink from a fountain enclosed that those outside do not taste; It does not spread outside nor draw from without. Those who are united in the flesh make but one soul and they raise a like spire of their piety by their mutual love. For marriage does not remove from God but brings all the closer to him because it is God himself who urges us to it.[1]

While his phrase "Those who are united in the flesh make but one soul" is but a poetic device, the existential unity effected between a man and a woman in the Sacrament of Holy Matrimony is, according to the Holy Apostle Paul, to be likened to the ineffable unity of Christ with His Church.[2] And both of these unities (that of Christ and His Church and that of husband and wife) have an eternal character.

Commenting on the phrase from the Church's Rite of Crowning, "Receive their crowns into thy Kingdom, preserving them spotless, blameless, and without reproach, unto ages of ages,"[3] the late priest, patristic scholar and theologian Protopresbyter John Meyendorff (1926-1992) wrote,

> "Herein lies the ultimate and true meaning of marriage as sacrament: whatever the difficulties, tragedies and divisiveness of human life on earth, crowns placed on the heads of two human beings are preserved in the Kingdom of God."[4]

This affirmation of the eternity of the marriage bond, reflected in the Holy Church's reticence to encourage the remarriage of widows and widowers,[5] is certainly at odds with the understanding

---

1   St Gregory of Nazianzus, On Virtue, Poem I, Section II, vv. 189-562; P.G., XXXVII, col 537-55.

2   Ephesians 5:20-33 which is read at the Rite of Crowning.

3   Prayer at the Removal of the Crowns at the conclusion of the Sacrament of Holy Matrimony.

4   John Meyendorff, Marriage: An Orthodox Perspective, St Vladimir's Seminary Press, New York, 1971, pp. 46-47.

5   Cf. I Corinthians 7:39 & 40.

of wedlock among non-Orthodox Christians which can be summarized by the familiar phrase "till death do us part."

In his letter of consolation to the widow of Therasios, St John Chrysostom (c. 347- 407) writes,

> You want to hear his voice, to enjoy his bright and noble presence and his love? Live in chastity, remain faithful to him even now that you are a widow, be eager to present a life worthy of him, and then you will go to the same place as he and will live with him in blessedness where is the choir of the saints, not for five or twenty or a hundred and a thousand or two thousand or ten thousand or many times as many years, but unto the infinite and endless ages.[6]

The eternity of the marriage bond is reflected in a folk tradition kept among pious Orthodox Christians: When one of the spouses departs this life, the ribbon connecting the two marriage crowns is severed so that the crown of the surviving spouse can be placed in the coffin of the departed spouse, while the crown of the departed spouse is retained to be placed at a later date in the coffin of the surviving spouse. It is believed then that each partner in the marriage reclaims his own crown in the Kingdom from the hands of his spouse where together they will live "in blessedness where is the choir of the saints ... unto the infinite and endless ages."

It is precisely because of the profundity of this eternal mystery of two becoming one flesh through Holy Matrimony that it is "meet and right" that it be entered into only after a period of prayerful discernment and spiritual preparation. We are grateful to our beloved and highly esteemed spiritual son Archpriest Josiah B.G. Trenham, PhD Dunelm, for providing to the Church his newest work "Enduring Love: Laying Christian Foundations for Marriage" in convenient workbook format. It is my sincere prayer that "Enduring Love" may be of immense assistance to the parish priest in his walk with engaged couples as they prayerfully discern and spiritually prepare for holy wedlock. May Father Josiah and this work be mightily blessed!

+BASIL
Retired Bishop of Wichita and the
Diocese of Mid-America,
Antiochian Orthodox Christian
Archdiocese of North America

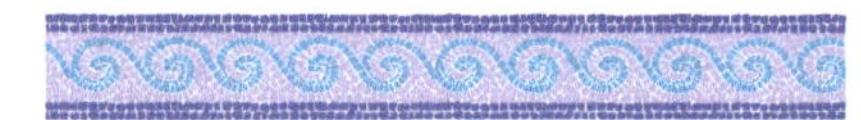

1. God's Design for Marriage

Marriage is God's

Marriage was not invented by man, but created by God. God fashioned marriage into the very nature of mankind, as an intrinsic part of what it means to be human. Marriage existed before cities, nations, or empires, and as such is pre-political: it is not the creation of politicians or governments, and as such cannot be altered by them. Marriage is God's, and God's alone. Because God is the author of marriage a Christian couple should pre-eminently ponder what God Himself desires from their marriage. This is the first concern of Christian couples, and their happiness flows from centering their marriage commitment in God.

God has fashioned marriage as a one-flesh union of man and woman that is **mysterious**, **unitive**, **monogamous**, **complimentary**, **indissoluble**, and **life-creating**. As such, marriage points beyond itself to God and His Kingdom. The Holy Prophet and God-Seer Moses describes the Lord God's fashioning of marriage in Genesis 2:18-25,

[18] Then the LORD God said, "It is not good that the man should be alone; I will make him a helper fit for him." [19] So out of the ground the LORD God formed every beast of the field and every bird of the air, and brought them to the man to see what he would call them; and whatever the man called every living creature, that was its name. [20] The man gave names to all cattle, and to the birds of the air, and to every beast of the field; but for the man there was not found a helper fit for him. [21] So the LORD God caused a deep sleep to fall upon the man, and while he slept took one of his ribs and closed up its place with flesh; [22] and the rib which the LORD God had taken from the man he made into a woman and brought her to the man.

[23] Then the man said,

"This at last is bone of my bones
and flesh of my flesh;
she shall be called Woman,
because she was taken out of Man."

[24] Therefore a man leaves his father and his mother and cleaves to his wife, and they become one flesh. [25] And the man and his wife were both naked, and were not ashamed.

Mysterious

There is more to marriage than meets the eye. St. Paul writes,

> For this reason a man shall leave his father and mother, and shall cleave to his wife, and the two shall become one flesh.' This mystery is great; but I am speaking with reference to Christ and the Church."[1]

Christian marriage is a sacrament, a holy mystery, designed to be a life-altering encounter with God Himself, a path of salvation, and of personal transformation. Just as the sacraments unite God and man, so too does marriage unite the couple both to each other and to God. Marriage isn't primarily about getting a license from the state, or a different tax status.

The Epistle Lesson read in the Crowning Service is from Ephesians 5:22-33. This text sets forth the reality that there are two marriages in the life of every believer: a spiritual marriage to Christ and an earthly marriage to one's husband or wife. Earthly marriage, the Great Apostle affirms, derives its contours and inspiration from the heavenly marriage (more on this in chapter 4, on Roles and Responsibilities). This text also raises the significance of marriage to great heights, by affirming that the divine drama of love between God and men is set forth visibly and publicly by the married lives of Christians, and in doing so, marriage reveals the Gospel to the world.

In the crowning service of an Orthodox Christian wedding, the Holy Gospel lesson read is from St. John 2. This text concerns the performance of Jesus' first public miracle at the Wedding Feast of Cana in Galilee. This text was chosen by the Church to be read at all weddings, not only to affirm the continuing validity of marriage for Christians in the New Covenant, but also to reveal that marriage becomes, in Christ, a place of miraculous transformations, in the same way that Christ transformed plain water into fine wine.

Elder Haralambos Dionysiatis, one of the great and Holy Elders of our times, bears witness to the amazing grace of the sacrament of marriage. This spiritual son of St. Joseph the Hesychast (+1959), teacher of noetic prayer, and Abbot of Dionysiou monastery on Mt. Athos, attended the weddings of his friends when he was in his early twenties. Reflecting on his experience at these weddings, he described himself as being overcome with emotion and ceaseless weeping sent from God. He would later say,

"I realized that it was from God. A wedding is a great Sacrament."[2]

All the Holy Mysteries of the Church are fashioned by God to affect a special union between God and men, and to save mankind. Marriage, as a Holy

---

1   Ephesians 5:31-32.

2   Monk Joseph Dionysiatis (2004) Abbot Haralampos Dionysiatis: The Teacher of Noetic Prayer, Monk Joseph Dionysiatis, Athens: Greece, pp. 40-41.

Sacrament, is designed for the salvation of the husband and wife. Marriage (together with the monastic estate) is the common context in which Christians work out their salvation. In the Divine Service, the first time the man and woman are mentioned by name is in the opening litany of the betrothal. The deacon intones,

"For the servant of God, N., and for the handmaid of God, N., who now pledge each other their troth,[3] and for their salvation, let us pray to the Lord."

Note that the first time the couple is mentioned by name is in a prayer for "their salvation", because Salvation is what Christian marriage is all about.

Unitive

In marriage a man leaves his father and mother, and cleaves to his wife, and the two become one flesh. God made Eve from Adam's rib – that is, from his own bones. The marriage of Adam and Eve was the closest of all earthly relationships. It was a true intertwining of being and purpose, designed by God to be a mystery revealing to human beings the relationship that Jesus Christ, the Bridegroom of the Church, has with His people, Christians. As such, since God Himself performs the marriage of His people, marriage effects a unity between the couple and God, and between the husband and wife themselves. The couple will always be the recipients of the mystery of marriage. They will also live the experience of being joined mystically together by God Himself, the mystery of being one flesh. For this reason, the Church forbids mixed marriage. Christians are not allowed to marry non-Christians.[4] Since marriage is a sacrament in which the bride and groom are united to

---

3   This old English word means "covenant" or "perpetual loyalty" and reflects the contractual nature of the betrothal service. In the Christian East marriage as a contract is expressed in the betrothal and the customs surrounding it, rather than in the vows of marriage as in the West.

4   Nor are Orthodox Christians permitted to marry non-Orthodox Christians except in certain circumstances (by economia), which are under the discretion of the ruling Bishop and the canons of the Church.

the Lord and to each other in God's Kingdom, the participants must previously be citizens of this Kingdom. The Rites of Initiation – baptism, chrismation and eucharist – not Crowning, is how someone enters the Kingdom the God.

Marriage was fashioned by God not only to join the man to the woman and the couple to God, but also to establish an unbreakable union between parents and children. A child born from the embrace of love in marriage is one flesh from two. The child is an eternal witness to the unity of his father and mother since every child is literally made of the same flesh as his parents, and nothing can eradicate this reality. The child may have his mother's nose, or his father's eyes, but however unique the child is, he in his one flesh is the expression of his parents' unity forever. The two have descended into one, and become three.

The unifying nature of marriage goes even further than this – it also establishes unity between families. This is one of the main reasons that the Lord God established sacred laws regulating who can wed, requiring that couples not be related by blood or baptism to certain degrees. These holy regulations (called the laws of consanguinity) are designed by God to further the unitive effect of marriage, spreading the familial bonds of love further out from the nuclear family to other families. Marriage therefore brings unity and peace to the culture.

The wisdom of God is magnificently expressed in the unitive power of marriage, since marriage, and marriage alone, joins together into a profound unity some of the most fundamental aspects of human life: sexual desire, love, commitment, home-life, child bearing, child rearing, bonds between families, and the creation of local culture. This is why the health of any people or nation can be measured by the health of its marriages.

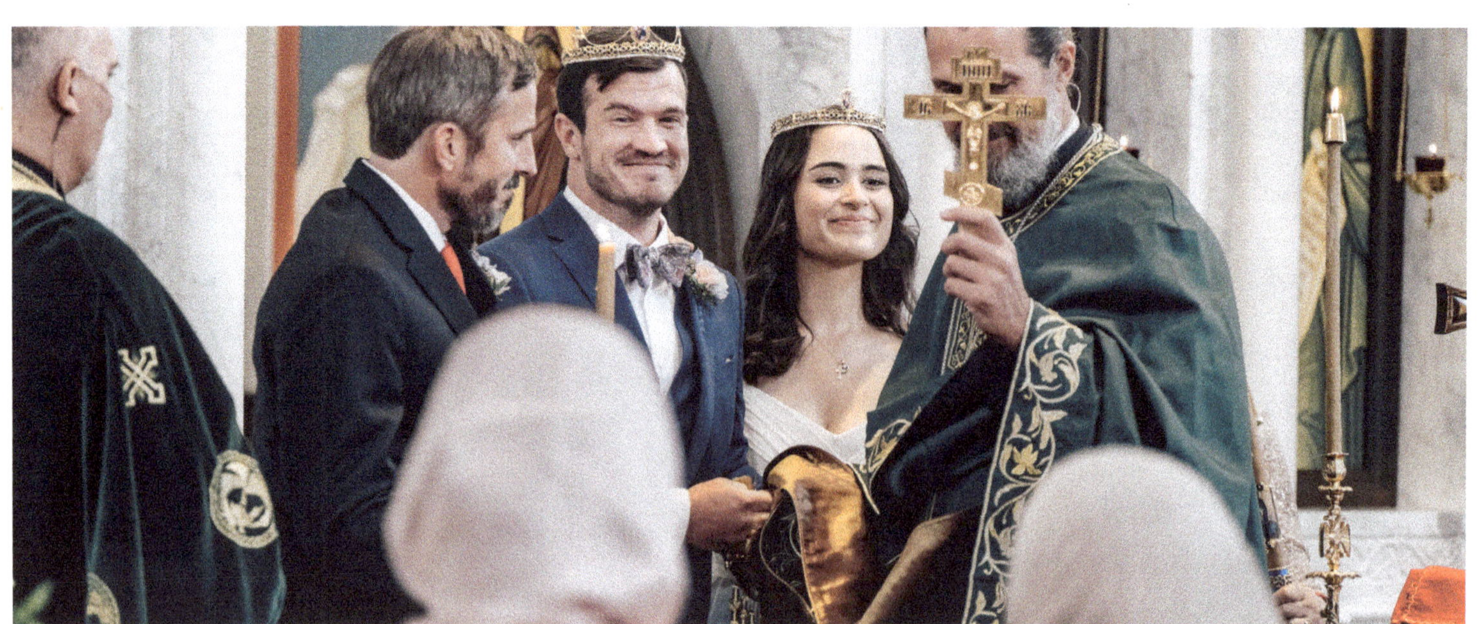

Monogamous

When God created marriage, He chose one man to marry one woman. Monogamy is an ordinance of creation. Polygamy, the practice of marrying more than one wife, was first practiced by the sinner Lamech as recorded in Gen. 4:19. God allowed this practice as a concession to the fallen and disordered state of man. Israel was surrounded by pagan peoples, some of whom married their own mothers and close relatives and practiced all sorts of sexual debauchery. For this reason God tolerated polygamy in the Old Covenant, even in the lives of His most celebrated servants like the Holy Patriarch Abraham and the great Prophet and King David. He made dispensation for polygamy while insisting on pre-marital chastity, the avoidance of marrying kin, and other upright sexual mores.

In the fullness of times, however, the Lord Jesus Christ became Incarnate, and abolished the divine concession of polygamy, as well as the concession for divorce, for his followers. The coming of Christ, and the salvation the Lord brought to mankind, has greatly elevated human potential and the standard of holiness that God expects from His people. It is written in St. Matthew's Gospel,

"They said to Him, 'Why then did Moses command to give her a certificate and divorce her?' He said to them, 'Because of your hardness of heart, Moses permitted you to divorce your wives; but from the beginning it has not been this way. And I say to you, whoever divorces his wife, except for immorality, and marries another woman commits adultery'" [5]

God's will for those whom He calls to marriage is that they marry one spouse, and live permanently with this spouse in love for the duration of one's earthly life, fashioning not only an earthly unity of body and of the home, but a unity of soul in love that will endure forever.

Complimentary

God fashioned mankind in two sexes: Male and Female. Man was created first, and woman was created out of man. This created origin reveals the essential unity of male and female, and their complementarity. There is no good male without the female. When God had fashioned all the animals for Adam, but Eve had not yet been created, Adam found himself alone. Adam had

---

no corresponding being, no authentic friend, no life companion, and no equal. He could speak but there was no partner to listen. He could love but there was no person to embrace. Up until this point, God had declared everything He created as "good", but He looked upon the state of Adam and declared it *not* good.[6] Therefore God made Eve, Adam's complement and completion. Then, and only then, did God declare creation "very good."[7] Man and woman were fashioned like a key and its lock: two pieces of a grand puzzle that fit together to make a whole. Just as a lock and key are each other's solution, so too are the man and the woman each other's solution. Wholeness and integrity are created in their one-flesh union, preserving chastity. The complimentary nature of marriage is more than just a biological or physiological reality, but a reality that involves the spiritual life and all the elements of who each person is: their dispositions, giftedness, leadership, service, and companionship. For this reason, Christian parents have always celebrated the marriage of their sons or daughters to be the great climax of their parenting, the great culmination of their labor to raise their children into God-loving adults. The Wise Sirach writes that parents who have joined their daughter in marriage have accomplished a "great task."[8]

Indissoluble

Marriage is a sacred contract, a public pledge of life-long fidelity, expressed in the promises made by the couple. These are traditionally expressed in the betrothal service and the surrounding customs of the Eastern Orthodox Church, and by the vows in the marriage service in the Western Christian denominations. However, marriage is much more than a contract. It is an indissoluble covenant of love, designed to be permanent, just as God's love is unending. Parents who resolve to live out the indissolubility of their marriage covenant provide their children great security and peace, and bear witness to God's faithfulness and enduring love. When a married couple divorces, the children witness the defilement of a holy sacrament and are deeply impacted, as their confidence in the power of love to endure is shattered.

Since marriage is a union of two becoming one, accomplished mysteriously by the hand of God Himself, the Church considers the severing of a marriage bond as tearing in half what God has united as one. It is a fighting against God. In Jesus' words,

"What God has joined together, let no man put asunder."[9]

The Prophet Malachi says, "God

---

6   Genesis 2:18

7   Genesis 1:31

8   Sirach 7:25

9   Mark 10:9

hates divorce."[10] Though divorce was permitted in the Old Testament, it was never God's will. Like polygamy, divorce was an accommodation by God to man's fallen condition before Jesus came and redeemed us. Today, Christians are forbidden to divorce, except for the most egregious and rare reasons. "No-fault" or easy divorce – which is so common today in the fallen and falling West – is abhorrent to God and the Church.

Life-Giving and Procreative

The unity of Adam and Eve in marriage was also designed to be fruitful in reproducing the image of God. The two became one in order to become three. God's first command to Adam and Eve was to be fruitful and multiply. Marriage is the means by which God's image is spread throughout the earth. After the Fall, the first description of married life is of Adam "knowing" Eve, and giving birth to children. Children are and have always been at the heart of married life, and are blessed. St. John Chrysostom calls procreation in marriage, "Sweet and universally desirable." St. Athanasius the Great writes, "Blessed is the man who, being freely yoked in his youth, naturally begets children." Though our culture has abandoned the traditional reverence for children and family life, the Church holds high the life-giving nature of marriage. The Christian family remains fecund wherever it finds itself, even in the dying

West: pious husbands and wives embrace the responsibility of parenthood that attends the enchanting pleasures of marital intercourse, because they do not separate what God has joined together: pleasure and childbearing.

As Such Marriage is Very Good

Genesis 1:31 reads,

> "And God saw all that He had made, and behold it was very good."

The fashioning of woman from man, and their joining into one flesh in marriage completes creation, manifests God's image and glory, and is the stage and means for fulfilling God's design for the whole earth.

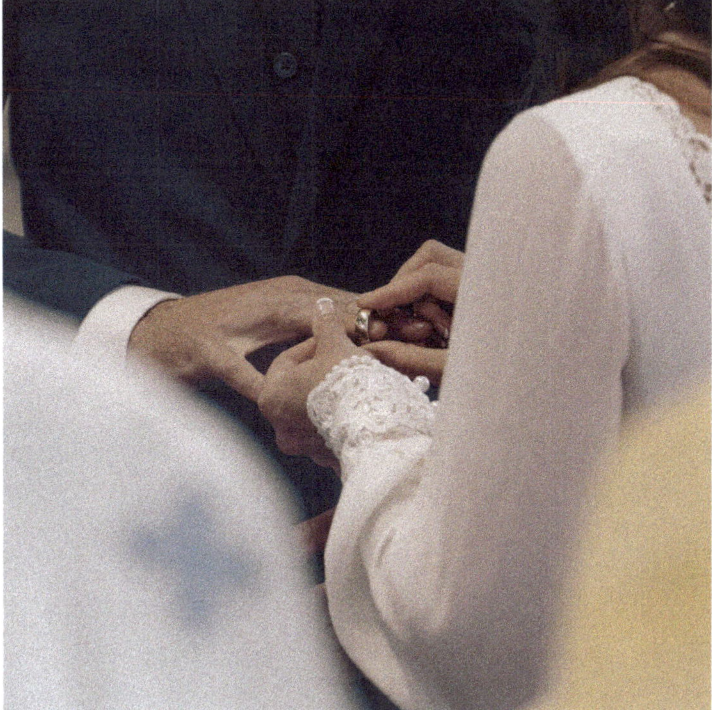

Discussion Questions

1 Why is it particularly important in today's world to reflect upon the fact that marriage is designed by God?

2 God says that marriage is "very good." How would your life be "not good" if you did not get married in general? What about to this particular person?

3 What do you hope to accomplish or what growth in virtue do you wish to obtain through marriage that you would not receive remaining single?

4 Why did you decide not to become a monk or nun? How will your salvation be furthered in marriage?

5 How will marrying your *specific fiancé* benefit your salvation?

Exercises

1 Write down your chief reasons for wanting to marry your betrothed.

2 Write down the chief reasons you think your intended wants to marry you.

3 List 3 unhealthy and erroneous reasons to get married.

2. Love and Expectations

Earthly Marriage as the Image of God's Love

Marriage is one of the most common recurring images throughout Holy Scripture. The Bible begins with God fashioning marriage between Adam and Eve, and ends with a marriage feast in heaven.

> "Hallelujah! For the Lord our God the Almighty reigns. Let us rejoice and exult and give him glory, for the marriage of the Lamb has come, and his Bride has made herself ready…Blessed are those who are invited to the marriage supper of the Lamb…And I saw the holy city, new Jerusalem, coming down out of heaven from God, prepared as a bride adorned for her husband; and I heard a loud voice from the throne saying, 'Behold, the dwelling of God is with men. He will dwell with them, and they shall be His people, and God himself will be with them; He will wipe away every tear from their eyes, and death shall be no more." [1]

Indeed, from Genesis to Revelation the Bible tells what is essentially the ultimate love story between God and His people, with God as the Bridegroom and His people as the Bride. Our Divine Husband, He celebrates over us with love. [1]

In the writings of the prophets, marriage is the most common metaphor used to describe the covenant relationship between the Lord God and His people. The Prophet Isaiah writes,

> "For your Husband is your Maker, the Lord of Hosts is His Name…the Lord has called you like a wife." Thus saith the Lord, "With everlasting love I will have compassion on you." [2]

And again Isaiah says,

> "As the bridegroom rejoices over the bride, so shall your God rejoice over you." [3]

The Prophet Jeremiah begins his prophecy the same way,

---

1   Rev. 19:6b-9a, 21:2-4a

2   Isaiah 54:5

3   Isaiah 62:5

"Thus says the Lord, 'I remember concerning you the devotion of your youth, the love of your betrothals as a bride." [4]

And again Jeremiah writes,

"Behold days are coming, declares the Lord, 'when I will make a new covenant with the house of Israel and with the house of Judah, not like the covenant which I made with their fathers in the day I took them by the hand to bring them out of the land of Egypt, My covenant which they broke, although I was a husband to them,' declares the Lord." [5]

This imagery continues throughout the rest of the Biblical text. In the Wisdom Literature the famous Song of Songs of King Solomon celebrates the union of God and His people as an erotic and conjugal love poem in which God says that His Bride has ravished His heart. The New Testament extends this nuptial imagery to describe the beginning of Jesus' holy ministry. St. John the Baptist says that he himself is not the Bridegroom, but the friend of the Bridegroom.[6] Jesus applies this image to Himself in His teaching. When He was criticized for not fasting with His disciples the Lord said,

"The attendants of the Bridegroom cannot mourn as long as the Bridegroom is with them, can they? But the days will come when the Bridegroom is taken away from them, and then they will fast." [7]

Jesus uses this imagery when He describes Himself as the Bridegroom that comes to take the Bride at midnight as an image of His Second Coming. The Bridegroom Orthros services of the first three days of Holy Week develop this in hymnody as the faithful sing,

"Behold the Bridegroom cometh at midnight, and blessed is the servant whom He shall find awake."

St. Paul, the Great Apostle, likewise describes his own ministry as a ministry of joining people to Christ in marriage. He tells the Corinthians,

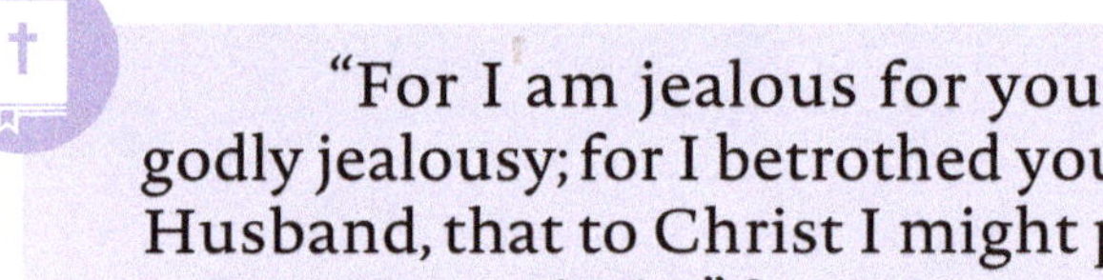

"For I am jealous for you with a godly jealousy; for I betrothed you to one Husband, that to Christ I might present you as a pure virgin." [8]

The love of God for His people is chiefly expressed in Scripture in the metaphor of marriage, but this meta-

<hr>

4 Jeremiah 2:2
5 Jeremiah 31:31-32
6 John 3:29
7 Luke 5:34-35
8 2 Cor. 11:2

phor goes both ways. Just as God's love for His people is expressed in the imagery of marriage, so too does the earthly marriage between a man and a woman serve as an icon of the great drama of love between God and His people. This is one very significant way that faithful marriages in every parish provide a living example of the Holy Gospel. Loving marriages are explosive forces for evangelism in every local parish.[9]

Perfect and Peaceful Love

St. John Chrysostom writes,

> "There is nothing which so welds our life together as the love of man and wife."[10]

In the opening litany of the Service of Betrothal, the couple is prayed for by name, and the clergy and faithful ask God to save them. Then the Church prays for their fruitful childbearing, and following this the litany continues with these words,

> "That God will send down upon them *perfect*, and *peaceful* love, and His help, let us pray to the Lord."

Perfect and peaceful love is what the entire Church supplicates God to give to the newlyweds. Love is the very air the couple should breathe. It is the sacred oil that allows the fellowship of marriage

to be sweet. Where is this love? It is the atmosphere of Paradise, the very stuff of heaven itself. This is why we ask God to "send it down" upon them. This is the love that is shared between the Father, the Son, and the Holy Spirit. This is the love that animates the angels and the saints in the Kingdom of God. It is the love that the Holy Spirit inspires in the hearts of all believers. It is to be the main characteristic of all Christians, and it is to be what chiefly binds together husband and wife. If the married couple is going to be saved together and if they are going to raise children for God they are certainly going to need love from God above all else.

Let's not leave this moving litany petition just yet. At the end of the petition for "perfect and peaceful love" we ask "God's help" for the couple. This beautiful phrase has its origin in the Maccabean history. In the 2nd century B.C., the pagan Greeks attempted to crush God's people Israel through the imposition of idol worship and the forbiddance of keeping the law of God. A group of faith-filled and valiant warriors called the Maccabees

---

9　The opposite is also true. A priest may preach the Gospel with great fervor and devotion, but if his parish is full of divorcees the hearers will not believe him.

10　Homily 20 on Ephesians; NPNF, Vol. 13, p. 143

arose to fight for God and against lawlessness. They were faith-filled freedom fighters whose godly deeds of courage are enumerated and celebrated in the pages of the Holy Bible.[11] Though these holy warriors faced tremendous odds they made each other strong by their mutual confidence in God and encouraged each other by using a common slogan. It consisted of two words that made all the difference in their fight for God: "God's help."[12] Those words are a watchword and a great encouragement to those striving to please God against great odds, and in the decadent West today any Christian couple striving to please God in their marriage will be struggling against great odds. With God's help your marriage can become an oasis of love.

The great 3rd century Church Father, St. Methodios of Olympus, describes marriage as an enchantment and an embrace of love. He writes,

"The ecstatic sleep into which God put the first man was a type of man's enchantment in love, when in his thirst for children he falls into a trance, lulled to sleep by the pleasures of procreation, in order that a new person…might be formed in turn from the material that is drawn from his flesh and bones…for man made one with woman in the embrace of love is overcome by a desire for children and completely forgets everything else." [13]

Types of Love in Marriage

In his famous 1958 text *The Four Loves*, C. S. Lewis unpacks the four classical types of love as understood in Greek. These are,

· Storge (στοργή), or affection, usually between family members
· Eros (ἔρως), or romantic love
· Philia (φιλία), or friendship
· Agape (ἀγάπη), or unconditional love; a love that abandons all for the sake of the beloved. This is the word used in 1 John of God Himself. God is love.[14]

All of these forms of love are to be manifest in Christian marriage, though they are not equally valuable, or valuable in every situation. Lewis points out the value of eros, for instance, as the passionate energy that gives a romance the fire or explosion that provides the initial momentum, like the fire that starts the

---

11   The longer canon of the Old Testament, found in both Orthodox and Roman Catholic Bibles, contains the books of the Maccabees. St. Paul also hymns the Maccabees in Hebrews 11.

12   2 Macc. 8:12 - θεοῦ βοηθείας

13   The Banquet of the Ten Virgins or Concerning Chastity, ANF, Vol. 6, pp. 313-314

14   1 John 4:8

engine of a train. Eros is the kind of love we commonly refer to in phrases like "falling in love." Eros is the initial spark that begins the journey towards and through marriage, but *eros* alone cannot sustain us on the journey. It is the same with the other loves – the affectionate love of *storge* and the friendship love of *philia* - all of these are natural and beautiful loves, but the love which unites and perfects them is agape. Agape is the kind of love that God has for us, and so Christian marriage cannot be perfected without it. The natural loves must therefore all prostrate before and be infused with *agape*.

 Agape has a particular relationship to expectations. *Agape* love enables expectations to bow before the sheer overwhelming beauty of God's love. It is the agape love of God, in the heart of the Christian husband and wife, that enables them to love each other *even when they do not like each other.* Trust me, there will be plenty of times when you do not like each other. *Agape* defies feelings. Nothing can stop it. It is the true mark of the Christian, according to the great St. Silouan the Athonite. It is the love that loves enemies, the love that Jesus manifested on His Precious Cross.

Marriage is the school of love.

The Lord Jesus summarized all of the commandments of God under the heading of two great commandments:

> Love the Lord your God with all your heart, and with all your soul, and with all your strength, and with all your mind; and love your neighbor as yourself.

These two commands summarize the two tables of the ten commandments: both our duty to God and our duty to human beings. When asked "Who is my neighbor?" Jesus responded by telling the parable of the Good Samaritan. The central theme of this parable is that your neighbor is "whoever in your life needs mercy from you." Husbands and wives who follow Jesus Christ learn to discern that their spouses are in fact their first

and chief neighbor, the neighbor that God Himself has provided so that they can learn to love the other as they love themselves.

Perfect and Peaceful Love is Indissoluble

The first prayer of the Service of Betrothal begins this way,

"O eternal God, who has brought into unity those who were sundered, and hast ordained for them an indissoluble bond of love...bless also these Thy servants."

The second prayer of the Service of Betrothal continues this theme,

"O Lord Our God, who hast espoused the Church as a pure Virgin from among the Gentiles: Bless this Betrothal, and unite and preserve these thy servants in peace and oneness of mind."

God's love, growing in the hearts of husband and wife, is what cements Christian marriage and preserves it as indissoluble. It is this love that denies separation, divorce and abandonment. It is this love that effects permanence.

Love is Action

All engaged couples should memorize 1 Corinthians 13:4-8, 13.

"Love is patient, love is kind, and is not jealous; love does not brag and is not arrogant, does not act unbecomingly; it does not seek its own, is not provoked, does not take into account a wrong suffered, does not rejoice in unrighteousness, but rejoices in the truth; bears all things, believes all things, hopes all things, endures all things. Love never fails...But now abide faith, hope, love, these three; but the greatest of these is love."

Here we see the content of the love we hope to fashion in marriage. Note that love here is *not a feeling*. There is nothing about emotions here. Rather, Scripture describes love using active verbs. Love is action. Love is selfless deeds, deeds made even more valorous if there are no emotive props, no deep feelings making them easy. Resolve to act lovingly in your marriage regardless of your feelings, and God will bless you mightily

Terms of Endearment

St. John Chrysostom in his sacred teaching on love between husbands and wives encourages husbands never to call their wives simply by their names, but with terms of endearment, honor and words that are pregnant with love and affection. Honor each other, he says, and you will not need honor from others. Give attention to and prefer each other above all others, and you will need no one else' attention or praise. In marriage we speak words of endearment to create and grow love, just as we speak words of thanksgiving to help fashion a grateful spirit, or speak the Jesus Prayer to cultivate a love for our Savior in our hearts. Words are very powerful. Words give grace or they can wound. We must therefore use them intentionally to nourish godly and loving marriages. Listen to St. Paul,

"Do not let any unwholesome word proceed from your mouth, but only such a word as is good for edification according to the need of the moment so that it may give grace to those who hear you."[15]

Mutual Forgiveness

Marriage is a workshop for the establishment of love in the hearts of the spouses, which in turn creates the atmosphere of the Christian home. The process necessarily involves heat. King Solomon writes in the Proverbs,

"As iron sharpens iron, so one man sharpens another."[16]

Think of this image of the blacksmith swinging his iron hammer and hitting the sword in the fire. Since marriage unites two *sinners*, marriage is at the same time often worked out in a context of tension, misunderstanding and spiritual failure. Homes can become domestic fiery furnaces. The great gift of Christian marriage is that the commit-

ment of the spouses is a commitment for life. Because it is indissoluble, it provides the time and opportunity for repentance, forgiveness and improvement.

A pilgrim once asked one of the Desert Fathers, "Elder, what do you monks do out here in the desert?" And the Geronda answered,

"We fall and get up. We fall and get up. We fall and get up again."

This is the same spiritual reality of Christian marriage. When a couple is dating they try to put on their best version of themselves, but marriage exposes all of our weaknesses, making conflict inevitable (see Ch. 4 "Communication and Conflict"). Spouses sin against each other every day, and the strong marriage is one in which both spouses learn how to say two things to each other every single day, "Forgive me, my love," and "God forgives and I forgive. Please forgive me also."

In our sacred monasteries the last prayer service of the day is the Little Compline service. At the conclusion of this service the superior of the monastery faces the monks or nuns and makes a prostration or bow saying, "Forgive me, a sinner." And then the monks or nuns respond by also making a prostration and saying, "Forgive me, a sinner." Orthodox Christian laity participate in something similar on "Forgiveness Sunday" to launch themselves into Great Lent. This universal and sacred ritual is a model for

---

15   Ephesians 4:29
16   Proverbs 27:17

all Christians on how to end the day, and a wise couple will end their evening prayer together by asking each other's forgiveness. This is a recipe for marital harmony and mutual love. Nothing makes sleep sweeter than when the couple blesses each other with the sign of the Precious Cross as they lie in bed having freshly forgiven each other.

True Love Means No Violence
St. John Chrysostom writes,

> "The partner of one's life, the mother of one's children, the foundation of one's every joy, one ought never to chain down by fear and menaces, but with love and good temper. For what sort of union is that, where the wife trembles at her husband? And what sort of pleasure will the husband himself enjoy, if he dwells with his wife as with a slave, and not as with a free-woman? Yes, though you should suffer anything on her account, do not upbraid her; for neither did Christ do this." [17]

Violence, physical altercations like pushing or slapping or threatening, has no place whatsoever in marriage. The couple is one flesh. The same care we show our own body we ought also give to the body of our spouse. Never allow yourselves to become violent for any reason whatsoever. Resolve never to commit this great sin.

Reasonable Expectations
Expectations for marriage vary widely between couples, and most of us form our own expectations for marriage from what we have seen in the lives of our parents. Some of us come from single family homes where marriage simply didn't exist. Since the sexual revolution of the 1960s, marriage has fallen on hard times and many young people have not grown up in homes with healthy marriages. Many have no examples of loving marital unions in their lives at all. Today in the United States marriage is no longer normative. Only a minority of houses are occupied by a husband, wife and children, a great demographic change from earlier in our culture. This change reflects a deep religious shift and a move away from the practice of the Christian faith. Parallel with the collapse of Christian marriage in the West, fantasy portrayals of relationships have flooded our media via film and fiction, but these portrayals frequently engender unreasonable expectations about marriage.

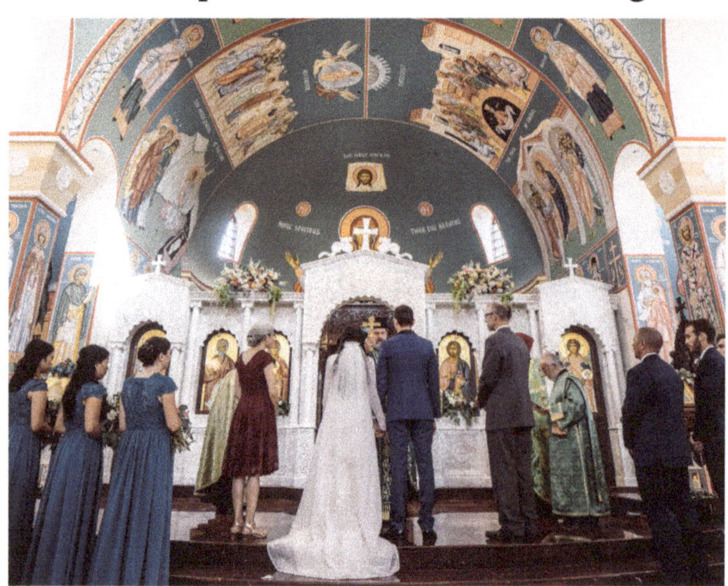

Reasonable expectations for marriage ought to be cultivated carefully in the garden of the Church. Those who seek to understand Christian marriage should study the beautiful marriages in Scripture, in the lives of married saints, and in the honorable married couples of one's own parish. In this way we can form the proper expectations of marriage.

How should one relate to the marriage of one's own parents? If your own parents were married but no longer are, then it is helpful to reflect upon their marriage in the same manner that we ought to reflect upon the life of a newly-deceased person at his funeral. At the funeral we should set aside any past grievances and consign those memories to the dustbin of forgetfulness. Instead, we should meditate upon any virtues in the life of the newly-departed and any beautiful memories, cherishing the memories and imitating the virtue, while forgetting the past grievances. In the same way, we ought to consign to history any bad aspects of the marriage of our parents, learning from these examples what we ought *not* replicate. We can then keep before our eyes those good examples of marriage in the lives of our parents, grandparents, godparents, and friends that will be edifying and inspiring to our own marriages. If your own parents were never married, then you can give thanks to God that, despite this, He has honored you with the great treasure of Christian marriage.

Discussion Questions

1 What are your expectations of yourself in your marriage?

2 What are your expectations of your spouse in your marriage?

3 What are your expectations of others towards your marriage?

Exercises

1 Reflect upon the marriage of your parents (if your parents were not married contemplate another marriage you know well). Discuss with your betrothed what you would like to imitate in that marriage, and what you would like to avoid.

2 If you come from a dysfunctional home, it is important to identify the nature of the dysfunction. What was it? How can you develop your marriage so as not to also manifest this dysfunction?

3 Write out your top 20 expectations of marriage. Review your list with the list your betrothed produced. Where do they overlap? Which ones are in only one list? Why?

(Continued on the next page)

Exercises

4 Most engaged couples, when asked why they were getting married would say, "Because we love each other." But is that true? Imagine that no couple in our country could get married unless they proved beyond a reasonable doubt that they loved the other person. Write what evidence you yourself would submit to the jury to prove that you love your betrothed.

5 Here is a list of unreasonable expectations for marriage: My betrothed will....

- Change his/her personality significantly after marriage
- Start to be spiritually serious after marriage
- Stop watching internet pornography after marriage
- Become financially responsible after marriage

Articulate several more unreasonable expectations for marriage. What makes an expectation reasonable or unreasonable?

Exercises

6 Think through one particular case imagining that this expectation was not being met. How might you respond in a constructive way?

7 Read 1 Cor. 13:4-8 together, and discuss how each of these definitions of love can be shown in your relationship. Apply these descriptions of love to your expectations. How can they show themselves?

8 Handling Disappointment: Share several of your greatest disappointments in your life with your betrothed, and reflect together on how you responded to these disappointments.

3. Friendship and Goals

Cultivating Marital Friendship

This chapter is dedicated to the great blessing of friendship between husband and wife, sacred companionship, the fellowship of life, marital collaboration, and the goals for marriage that flow from such blessed concord. Friendship cannot be forced, only chosen. The great honor of being married is that your spouse has freely chosen you above all others to have and to hold forever. Marital friendship is like art or the universe itself since it does not arise from necessity but from free choice. The profound union of marital friendship is hymned throughout the wedding service as the church repeatedly prays in numerous instances for concord of soul and body, for peace and concord, for oneness of mind, for harmony, and for the bond of peace.

The deep and settled attraction between a man and a woman, and its consummation in God-ordained and God-blessed marriage, should cause us all to stand in stunned amazement and appreciation of such beauty. Jesus, the son of Sirach, writes,

> "My soul takes pleasure in three things, and they are beautiful in the sight of the Lord and of men: agreement between brothers, friendship between neighbors, and a wife and husband who live in harmony."[1]

Agreement, friendship, and harmony between a husband and his wife are beautiful in the sight of the Lord.

Likewise, King Solomon says,

> "Here are three things too wonderful for me, four that I cannot understand: the way of an eagle in the sky, the way of a snake on a rock, the way of a ship at sea, and the way of a man with a maiden."[2]

These Scriptural expressions of awe at the mystery of the union between a man and a women existed even before Christ came into the world and made the

---

1   Sirach 25:1
2   Proverbs 30:19

world new. Since the coming of Christ, the union between a man and a woman in marriage has been greatly elevated and ennobled, for it has been infused with the very presence of the Kingdom of God.

Face-to-face friendship with God is the highest calling of man. It was Adam's mode of being in Paradise. It was the gift of God to the Holy Patriarch Abraham to be called "God's friend."[3] It was the honor given to the Holy Prophet and God-Seer Moses to be called "God's friend."[4] It was also the joy of the Much-Suffering Prophet Job to have God's friendship.[5] It is the prized possession of disciples of Jesus that He should call us His "friends."[6] The highest form of friendship is between human beings and God, and the friendship between husband and wife imitates and serves as an icon for this friendship between God and man. Christian marriage, therefore, is intended to be an earthly type of this divine-human union, and a witness to the divine-human friendship that God has made possible with humanity through His Son, Jesus Christ. This is why one of Christ's titles in the Church is "the Friend of mankind."

God our Father has always dwelled in an eternal communion of love with His Only-Begotten Son, Jesus Christ, and His Holy Spirit. Man, fashioned in the image of God, is made for communion with God and with other human beings. We are communal beings, and the intimate communion of marriage is designed by God as built into the very fabric of human existence. Those that the Lord God has called to marriage know it by the yearning they have for deep communion with another human being. Deep friendship in marriage is something that must be nourished and cultivated over time.

The "Not-Good" of Paradise

St. Tikhon, the Patriarch of Moscow, writes,

> Without a helpmate the very bliss of paradise was not perfect for Adam: endowed with the gift of thought, speech, and love, the first man seeks with his thought another thinking being; his speech sounds lovely and the dead echo alone answers him; his heart, full of love, seeks another heart that would be close and equal to him; all his being longs for another being analogous to him, but there is none…then the bountiful God, anxious for the happiness of man, satisfies his wants and creates a mate for him – a wife. But if a mate was necessary for man in paradise, in the region of bliss, the mate became much more necessary for him after the fall, in the vale of tears and sorrow.

---

3   2 Chronicles 20:7

4   Exodus 33:11

5   Job 29:4

6   John 15:15

Adam's early existence in Paradise caused a strange paradox: Adam was in Paradise but there was something that was "not good." Paradise is supposed to be all good, yet the Paradise of God's creation suffered because it was incomplete. Paradise lacked woman. Adam lacked his compatriot, his equal, his partner. The Lord God, ever seeking the blessing of man, solved the dilemma. God's solution is recounted in the second Crowning Prayer of the wedding service,

> "In the beginning Thou didst make man and set him to be King over Thy creation, and didst say: It is not good for man to be alone on the earth; let us make a helpmate for him; Taking one of his Ribs, Thou didst fashion Woman, which when Adam beheld, he said, 'This is now bone of my bone, and flesh of my flesh; she shall be called Woman.'"

The Preacher in Ecclesiastes writes,

> "Two are better than one because they have a good return for their labor. For if either of them falls, the one will lift up his companion. But woe to the one who falls when there is not another to lift him up. Furthermore, if two lie down together they keep warm, but how can one be warm alone? And if one can overpower him who is alone, two can resist him. A cord of three strands is not quickly torn apart."[7]

This marvelous text bears witness to how marital friendship nourishes our mutual needs. Learning to partner together to meet each other's needs for love, warmth, health, intimacy, and fellowship is the path of marriage.

The Common Cup

One of the most significant rituals in the Crowning Service comes just after the recitation of the Lord's Prayer and just before the triple procession around the marriage table. It is the blessing and reception of the "common cup." Its significance is profound. The couple starts by praying the "Our Father" for the first time as married persons, and in this prayer they ask God to bring His Kingdom and His will to the earth and into their own lives. In this prayer, the couple also asks God not to lead them into temptation but to deliver them from evil.

Having prayed this, they next *receive* God's special blessing found in the common cup. The common cup, which has just been blessed by the celebrant, is not a remnant of the eucharist, nor a stand-in ritual for former days when marriages were often celebrated in the

---

7   Ecclesiastes 4:9-12

middle of the Divine Liturgy. Even when a crowning is performed in the middle of the Divine Liturgy there is still the blessing and reception of the common cup in addition to the reception of the Holy Eucharist. The reception of the common cup is a sacred act in which God blesses the couple with the sweetness of His gifts, and the couple agrees to embrace the future together no matter what comes. They engage the good and bad, sickness and health, prosperity and need, *together*. They drink all of life from *one cup*. Their future will be common because they are one. And the first thing that this newly united couple experiences as married persons is the sweetness of God's blessing. Not only do they taste sweet wine in drinking the common cup of sufferings of this life, but the priest also prays for them in the second Crowning Prayer that the gladness which St. Helen had when she found the Precious Cross might come upon them. With God's blessings, both drinking the cup of sufferings and bearing the Cross of the Lord together can be blessed with peace and gladness.

Togetherness Always and in Every Place

When two individuals are united in the community of marriage they are changed in their very mode of being. They are no longer individuals, they are married persons. To understand this radical change that takes place in marriage, it is helpful to meditate upon the miracle of the ordination of a priest. When a man is set aside by the church for ordination to the sacred priesthood he is removed from amongst the laity, and by his ordination he becomes an ecclesial person. He assumes a beautiful new relationship to everyone in the church. He becomes a spiritual father, and relates as such to all his parish, old and young, men and women. Suddenly, all of their cares, concerns and interests are his. The new priest opens his heart to receive within it every person equally in his parish. This new mode of being is established in reality by the laying-on of hands by the bishop, but it is established in practice by the priest learning to live according to what he has become: a man of God and a man of the Church.

Just as a new priest has to learn to live according to his new reality, so newlyweds need to learn to live according to *their new reality of married existence*. This takes concerted effort and focus because it is a completely new way of life. Newlyweds do not simply have a new relationship between themselves, but all their other relationships become new. They have a new relationship to their parents. They have a new relationship to their friends. They have a new relationship to the public. These new relationships have to be intentionally formed, crafted by the couple's will. It is not easily done.

They have to learn not to keep secrets since their minds don't belong to themselves alone but to their spouses. They have to change their vocabulary, abandoning the words "mine" and "yours" since their possessions don't belong to themselves alone but also to their spouses. They have to learn to care for their bodies, to eat and drink responsibly, to exercise, to sleep sufficiently, and to serve in a new way, whether they feel like it or not since their bodies no longer belong to themselves alone but to their spouses. Wherever a husband goes he goes there as a married man. He bears his wife with him in his heart and mind. Wherever a wife goes she goes there as a married woman. She bears her husband with her in her heart and mind. Their souls are entangled and though their bodies are distinct, they are not ultimately separate.

Marriage as a Plant

The beautiful relationship of marriage can be conceived of as a marvelous plant given to the couple by God Himself. God has fashioned the plant, but as having received a divine gift the couple themselves must care for the plant. For the plant to grow and bear sweet fruit it must be nourished. It must be properly watered. It must be exposed regularly to the sun. It must sometimes be fertilized. Its leaves must sometimes be trimmed. Weeds in its soil-bed must be pulled. This is simply how a precious plant is cared for. On top of this regular care, the basic maintenance of the Holy Sacrament of Marriage, a newly married couple is like a new plant that has not yet had the time and experience to establish deep roots, and therefore must be shown special care. Once a plant has had time to lay deep roots into the soil, it can suffer foul weather much more easily than when it is young and vulnerable. In the Old Testament, newly-wed husbands were exempted from military service for the first year of marriage for exactly this reason: to give the new couple time to grow and put down roots. It is therefore important to establish the sacred routines that nourish marriage, especially in the first year.

Date Night and Relationship Priorities

There are many enemies to marital intimacy and deep friendship. One of the most common enemies sneaks up because it doesn't appear to the couple to be an enemy. This enemy is the improper presence of children in the family home. Children are born as the fruit of the love of married couples. The children stand forever as witnesses to the loving embraces of the parents. Parenting can be so challenging and wonderful and all-consuming that many couples allow the task of parenting to push aside the priority of spending private one-on-one time together. Unexpectedly the marriage bond itself can be neglected and marital friendship starved and damaged. It is of supreme importance to remember that one was a husband or wife *before* one was a father or mother.

Maintaining relationship priorities is key to the success of marriage and family life. The first relationship that must be maintained as primary is the relationship of the husband and wife individually with the Lord God. He is to be the "first love" of all His people.[8] A husband is usually a disciple of Jesus Christ *before* he becomes a husband, and the priority of his relationship with Jesus must be maintained.[9] It is by maintaining the supremacy of Jesus Christ in his life that the husband can actually be a good and Christian husband. A father was a husband *before* he became a father, and the priority of his relationship with his wife must be maintained. It is by maintaining the supremacy of his wife in his life that the father can actually be a good father to his children and show his children the glory of married love. For children to know that the *first earthly love* of their parents is for each other is a great gift to children. This is how children themselves can assume a great appreciation for marriage itself and desire it for themselves.

One of the most practical ways for husbands and wives to live this way is to maintain a date night each week, unalterable except by emergency. This means the husband and wife regularly spend time together *apart from the children*. Mature marriages keep date nights without question. Another important way to nourish the intimate friendship of marriage is for the husband and wife to maintain their bridal chamber as off limits to children. Children should not be allowed to regularly sleep in the marriage bed of their parents. This is an improper invasion of

---

8   Rev. 3:17
9   This is not true, of course, for those who become Christians after marriage.

marital intimacy. A certain awe should be inculcated in children for their parents' marriage bed as the place where by God's blessing they were themselves brought into life.

Setting Goals for Marriage

It is rightly said that we fail at 100% of the goals that we never set. Setting goals is a means of dignifying a calling, of expressing the seriousness with which we take our lives. Fixing goals helps to focus energy and to bring forth precious accomplishments. All Christians share the ultimate goal of loving God and entering into His eternal Kingdom. Married Christians share common goals about fashioning their marriages into an earthly picture of the relationship between Jesus and the Church. In marriage, we all are called to the goal of manifesting the transformative power of the Lord to turn the water of our lives into the wine of His grace. Besides common goals, each marriage is the exceptional union of two unique persons. As such, no two couples have the same goals. Fashioning goals together in marriage is a beautiful way to nourish friendship and a common life. Ultimately setting goals is a means to further personal change, to call ourselves to become what we need to become to serve God and the ones we love. On the following page are a number of exercises to guide you in setting common goals for your marriage.

Discussion Questions

1 If marriage forms a new reality of togetherness, a new mode of being "married persons", how does being married change the way one might interact in various situations? In public? Around members of the opposite sex? In work settings? Around parents and in-laws?

2 If the sacrament of marriage can be compared to a plant, how might a couple make sure their "marriage-plant" might get sun?

3 What could be some common "weeds" that would need to be regularly extracted from the soil of the marriage?

4 How could the "marriage-plant" be fertilized?

Exercises
The Marriage Goals Pie

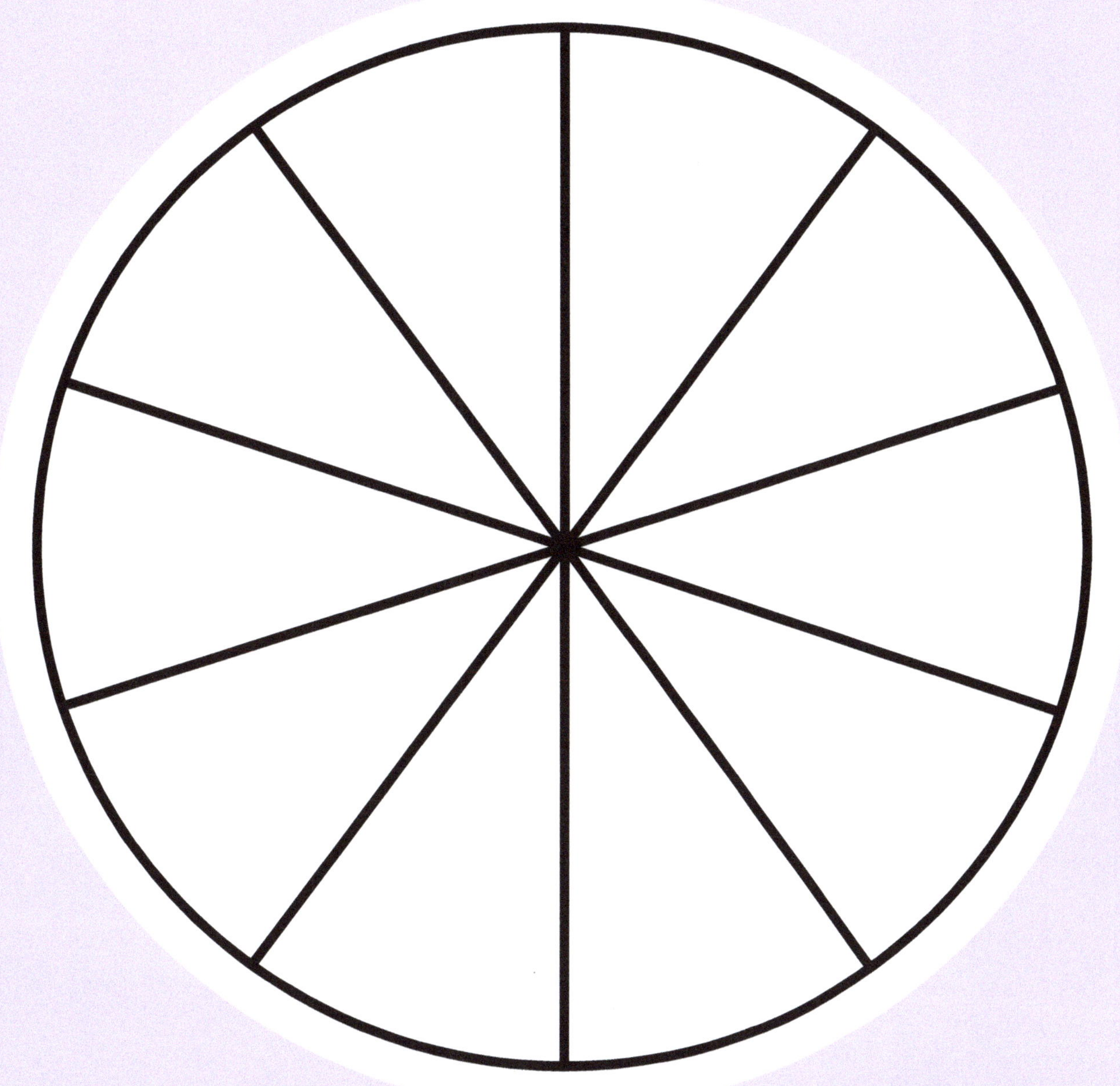

1 As a collaborative exercise in establishing goals together, write a marriage goal in each of the ten pie sections.

(Continued on the next page)

Exercises

1 Prioritize the top 5 goals and number them #1 to #5 by mutual agreement.

2 Each of you choose one goal that you could live without.

3 Place a star (*) next to any goal you think you learned from your parents.

4 Flesh out a practical step-by-step plan to accomplish the top two goals.

5 Agree upon a time when you will reevaluate your goals together in the future. You may wish to consider doing this on the occasion of each of your wedding anniversaries.

4. Communication and Conflict

Communication

Healthy and loving communication is absolutely central to the development of marital friendship. Significant communication brings many other benefits to marriage including protecting the spouse from loneliness, maintaining and deepening trust, comforting children, and reducing anxiety as it is said that shared burdens are halved. Poor communication fosters exactly the opposite: more stress, loneliness, insecurity, and anxiety. Communication is hugely important in marriage. According to studies, not being able to talk sufficiently with one's spouse is a major contributing factor to divorce.

The word "communication" shares its root with the word "commune" that we Christians so love. It comes from a Latin root, *communicare*, and according to the Oxford English dictionary its meanings include: to share, to impart, to convey, to transmit, to make common with another, to use or enjoy in common with, to gain mutual understanding, even to have sexual intercourse with. Specifically, in a liturgical context, to commune means to receive Holy Communion. Only a rich tapestry of imagery like this can capture the breadth of what communication means.

We confess that God Himself lives in an eternal communion of love with His Only-Begotten Son and His Holy Spirit. We confess that the Holy Trinity has invited us human beings and sinners into this communion of love. Jesus has summoned us to be joined to Him, and to share His intimate and filial relationship with His Father. Jesus is God's only Son *by nature*, but Jesus has invited us to His Body the Church in order to share by grace in the union with His Father that He has by nature. In Christ we become sons and daughters of God. The Church is a communion of love between the Holy Trinity and the children of God. We renew this communion whenever we receive the Holy Eucharist. It is the very center of our worship life. God nourishes us in our communion with Him by the Holy Mysteries of the Church and by His Holy

Word. He speaks to us. He touches us. He embraces us. He dwells within us. Word and Sacrament are God's love languages. This is how He communicates Himself to us. By His providential care He nourishes us. By His creation He delights us. He has placed man at the center of His vision. He has fixed His eyes upon us. The Church of the Living God is the family of God, and it has the mission to reveal, nourish, guard, and advance love.

Christian marriage is a communion of persons with the same calling. Christian homes are to be domestic churches where love is revealed, guarded and communicated. The two spouses become one, and this oneness is to be the hallmark of Christian marriage. It is to be oneness not just of body but also of mind. This is why we pray throughout the Crowning Service for peace, concord of body, harmony of soul, and *oneness of mind.* These are gifts of personal communion, and are gifts to be cultivated, nourished, and deepened. Every couple, inspired by

God's own pursuit of us, is to pursue each other in love. Each husband and wife has their time together to fashion numerous expressions of love and communication. We must learn to speak each other's languages of love. We ought to learn to do that which delights the Beloved. We are resolved to communicate our love as God has communicated His: by condescension, by words, by counsel, by sympathy, by relief, by foot-washing, by deeds of service, by gifts, by personal offering, by listening, by touch, by embrace, by a smile, by our eyes, by the hand, and by sacrifice unto death, which is the highest form of love. St. John Chrysostom teaches that marital communication should be infused with tender love and sacrifice. He writes,

> "Whenever you give your wife advice, always begin by telling her how much you love her. Nothing will persuade her so well to admit the wisdom of your words as her assurance that you are speaking to her with sincere affection. Tell her… that you love her more than gold…Take the same provident care for her, as Christ takes for the Church. Yea, even if it shall be needful for thee to give thy life for her, yea, and to be cut into pieces ten thousand times, yea, and to endure and undergo any suffering whatever – refuse it not."[1]

Human communication consists of words, tone, and non-verbal communication via body-language. These three components of communication are all important. Content, or what words are actually said, is important, and how it is

---

1   Homily 20 on Ephesians, NPNF, Vol. 13, p. 144.

said – both the tone in which it is said and additional body language – all are packed with meaning. Meaning is thought to be primarily communicated through nonverbal cues and tone, even more than verbal content. Miscommunication is common when these three aspects appear to the spouse to be in conflict. When a wife comes in from outside to share some exciting news with her husband who is reading on his iPad and she says, "Guess what honey! My roses are blooming!" and the husband doesn't look up from his iPad but says, "That's great sweetheart, I'm so happy for you", the wife may simply not believe him. He said the right thing, but the other modes of communication – his tone and body language – told a completely different story that won the day. He is so incredibly happy that he just can't stop reading the news. She gets it. Quality communication presupposes not just content, tone, and the non-verbal, but also requires a deep resolve to speak and to listen. Sometimes, for husbands especially, this has to be learned; it doesn't just happen. Harmonizing our words, tone, and non-verbal communication in order to cooperatively convey our true message is the path to mature communication.

The Proverbs of Solomon give sound counsel on how to combine wise words with helpful tones and non-verbal communication. Some 15% of the Proverbs is dedicated to how to have wise speech. King Solomon is clear that the prerequisite for wise speech is a pure heart that fears God.

"A wise man's heart guides his mouth."[2]

He provides teaching about the importance of thinking before speaking:

"The heart of the righteous weighs its answers, but the mouth of the wicked gushes evil." [3]

He provides teaching about showing proper restraint in words:

"A man of knowledge uses words with restraint...he who holds his tongue is wise."[4]

He provides teaching about averting unnecessary confrontation:

"A gentle answer turns away wrath, but a harsh word stirs up anger." [5]

We are counseled to avoid speech that is harsh, rash, vile, impatient, false, and crude. Instead, we are to clothe our words in gentleness, soothing, appropriateness, sincere intention, righteousness, patience and circumspection. Professor John Gottman, psychologist and well-known relationship researcher, has articulated a pattern that he has found in his more than four decades of researching marital stability. He calls it the Magic Relationship Ratio 5:1. For every one

2   Proverbs 16:23

3   Proverbs 15:28

4   Proverbs 17:27a, 10:19b

5   Proverbs 15:1

shared negative communication between spouses, joyful and stable marriages share five positive interchanges.

Conflict

Generally speaking there are two types of conflict: conflict that arises by the will of God, and conflict that arises by our own sins.

There are many divine purposes served by the Lord God in allowing conflict into the lives of His children. Our Lord Jesus Christ, the Lord of Love and the Prince of Peace, nevertheless endured gargantuan amounts of conflict in His earthly life. As an infant, His life was threatened by Herod's murderous intents. In the recesses of the desert just prior to the launching of our Savior's public ministry, He entered into conflict with the devil himself. Over the three year course of His ministry of preaching, teaching, healing, and exorcism, Jesus endured repeated conflict with the devils, with the Pharisees, Sadducees and Scribes, with the Jewish Sanhedrin, and sometimes even with His own faithless disciples. These conflicts in our Savior's life constituted a portion of His Precious and Life-Giving Cross, and demonstrate in absolutely unique ways His immense love, patience, and wisdom. Conflict was opportunity for the revelation of the Lord's glory, and so it is in the lives of His faithful disciples.

The Holy Apostles imitated the Lord. A servant is not above His Master;

as the Master endured conflict so it is inevitable that those who faithfully serve Him will endure conflict with the world, the flesh, and the devil. St. Paul writes,

> "For to you it has been granted not only to believe in His Name but to suffer for His sake."[6]

Suffering means more than suffering external conflict, but not less. Suffering conflict for Jesus' sake is the honorable lot of Christians.

Besides the conflict that arises by the will of God – which is to be welcomed with faith – we also experience conflict that is born of sin: our own sin and that of others. Since our Lord is sinless He never caused unnecessary conflict, but He certainly endured conflict born of the sins of others. The Holy Apostles, especially when they were young and inexperienced in faith before Holy Pentecost, precipitated conflict amongst themselves by their own selfish ambitions. They disputed with each other about who was the greatest. Even the Foremost of the Apostles, Ss. Peter and Paul, experienced conflict about exactly how to conduct their ministries properly. The New Testament is full of examples of conflicts born of sin in the lives of the disciples. Just think of the conflicts in the Church of Corinth born of hero-worship and social prejudice or the conflict amongst the widows in the Church of Jerusalem born of ethnic division. These sinful conflicts grieve the Holy Spirit, and damage the witness of the Church since these conflicts bear witness to a lack of Christ-like love.

The more Christians deepen their love for God and others, the less they are involved in sinful conflicts. St. James, the Brother of the Lord, writes,

> "What is the source of quarrels and conflicts among you? Is not the source your pleasures that wage war in your members? You lust and do not have; so you commit murder. And you are envious and cannot obtain; so you fight and quarrel. You do not have because you do not ask." [7]

Quarrels and conflicts arise from our passions. Christian maturation is a process of conquering the passions and cultivating the virtues. In this context, we can see clearly how the greatest contribution any spouse can make to marital harmony is deepening his or her spiritual life. Increasing the size of our hearts

for God is the greatest gift we can give to our spouses and children. Since so many conflicts are rooted in sin, it is also clear that no techniques are going to establish peace if your spiritual life is not cultivated. There is no substitute for love. All efforts to improve communication and eliminate sinful conflicts are doomed to fail without love that comes from the grace of God.

Fighting Fair

Like the disciples of old we Christians today are living a divided existence. The Kingdom of God is here already in our lives, but not yet in fullness. We are already redeemed in Christ, but not completely. We have salvation, but are still working that salvation out. We are new creations in Christ, but the old man is not yet fully extinguished. The Resurrection is still before us, and it is not until that glorious eschatological moment that we will be forever delivered by our passions and enter into the Kingdom of God and become immune from all sinful conflicts.

In the meantime, we believers must learn to endure each other and even ourselves patiently. Spouses are meant to grow in their love over time. They learn to have compassion for each other's sinful tendencies and weaknesses. We learn to cover a multitude of each other's sins with the blanket of love. [8] We learn to be patient with each other since we

---

7   St. James 4:1-2
8   St. James 5:19-20

ourselves are hard to live with. Growing humility brings growing peace. Nevertheless, sometimes, even in the strongest marriages, serious conflicts arise. What are we to do then? How can we keep the fire of conflict from escalating into a firestorm that does permanent damage?

Couples must learn how to fight fair. This is not a way of saying that fighting is tolerable. Fighting is not OK, and if we have more love and more holiness we wouldn't fight each other. Learning to fight fair is wise. It is a way to limit the damage of an unfortunate reality, and possibly to turn it into something constructive. The rules of a fair fight in boxing are formally established. One of those rules – there is no hitting below the belt – has become a symbol of fair fighting in general in our culture. Something that is "below the belt" is something unacceptable in any circumstance. It is egregious and cannot be tolerated even in a conflict of fighting. Married couples are wise to lay the groundwork early in their marriage about fair conflict. They should agree upon what exactly is below the belt,

and what they will simply never say or do. If one or both of the spouses hit below the belt there is an immediate cessation. There is no benefit to continue until the one who has committed the egregious infraction owns up to it, and acknowledges that there is no reason to go on until he or she sincerely apologizes for undermining the very possibility of resolution. That is the only way to go on.

Father Josiah's 14 Rules for Fighting Fair

1. Don't use the "D" word (divorce) as a threat
2. Don't be physically abusive
3. Don't be verbally abusive or call names
4. Don't interrupt constantly
5. Don't involve someone else in the conflict without mutual consent
6. Don't withhold sex from your spouse as a punishment
7. Don't bring up the past as proof that the other will "never change"
8. Don't generalize and turn a conflict about specifics into generalization
9. Don't let the sun go down on your anger
10. Don't bring the children into it
11. Don't fight in front of others
12. Don't continue if you are too weary
13. Don't reject compromise
14. Don't give up and withdraw

Emotions

Often at the center of conflict are our emotions. Emotions are a gift from God and part of what it means to be a human being. To be able to feel, to experience happiness and sadness, joy and sorrow, motivation and repulsion, delight and grief, are all part of the mystery of human existence. As sinners, however, our emotions are disordered, and while sometimes our emotions support our intended actions of love and service it is also true that sometimes our emotions are great obstacles to doing the right thing. Emotions can sometimes support our marriages but can sometimes undermine them. Emotions must be evaluated and not simply given in to. They must be tamed. They must be made to submit.

There is a simple rule we can follow with regards to emotions. When our emotions support us in doing the will of God we can give thanks for this and our wills can find additional support or back-up from our emotions. When we have deep feelings of compassion, this can help us to serve the needy. On the other hand, when our emotions oppose or hinder us in doing the will of God, we should studiously despise our emotions.

It is especially at these times that our good deeds are most valuable and are shown to be valuable acts of Christian decision. The Lord Jesus teaches that it is easy to love those who love us. Even the heathen do this. But to love those who are your enemies, to serve those who use us is a uniquely Christian action, and to do this is to show ourselves to be authentic children of God Himself, Who causes His sun to rise upon both the wicked and the good. Very few people are sufficiently holy to have emotions that support the action of loving enemies. When faced with such a circumstance, our Lord Christ calls us to crucify our emotions, and to love the enemy. Mature Christian believers have nourished strong wills. They are steady and dependable because their actions are not dependent upon their emotions. Learning to love and serve your spouse in marriage, regardless of your emotions, is the path of marital holiness.

Exercises

1 Write your own rules for fair fighting.

____

____

____

____

____

2 Number them according to seriousness with #1 being the most important.

3 All of us have mechanisms that we use to cope with conflict and tragedy. List below five healthy coping mechanisms and five unhealthy coping mechanisms. Try to focus on your own actual mechanisms.

	Healthy	Unhealthy
1	_______________	_______________
2	_______________	_______________
3	_______________	_______________
4	_______________	_______________
5	_______________	_______________

Exercises

4

*Conflict Styles Chart**

The bottom styles of withdraw and win are base approaches to conflict. Neither are helpful. Those who primarily withdraw are hopeless. Those who must always win are self-centered. The top styles are more dignified. Yielding, when not involving a fundamental principle, can express humility and promote reconciliation. Resolving expresses free and open communication. Compromise is the central goal. When two must live in oneness this means a common center is negotiated and agreed upon which is neither one spouse's nor the other spouse's specific desires, but a unified goal agreed upon by both.

Yield	**Resolve**
Compromise	
Withdraw	**Win**

* This chart is taken from James Fairfield (1977)
When You Don't Agree, Scottdale, PA: Herald Press

(Continued on the next page)

Exercises

5 What are each of your particular styles of conflict resolution?

6 Describe a scenario where yielding would be virtuous.

7 Describe a scenario where winning would be disastrous.

Scenarios

8 Describe a real scenario where you and your partner successfully compromised. How has this been a blessing?

9 After 10 years of marriage John tells his counselor, "I no longer have feelings for my wife, Julie. Don't get me wrong. She is a good wife, and a fine mother. I admire her, but I am not in love with her anymore. I actually have more feelings for my old girlfriend from high school. I can't imagine going on like this. It is like I am denying my true feelings." John is wondering if and how he can regain his feelings for his wife. Julie is wondering what has happened, and what she could have done to cause this.

What are the possible causes of their problems, and how could they move forward?

(Continued on the next page)

Scenarios

Read Rev. 2:4-5 where a similar scenario is taking place in spiritual marriage. What does Jesus counsel us when we "lose our feelings" for Him?

10 Max and Irene have been married for 15 years, and have three children. Recently Max has become increasingly withdrawn, and Irene has become suspicious. She discovered on his phone and computer that Max has been watching hours of pornography every day. Irene confronted Max for his infidelity, and Max responded that it was just "computer women" and not real. Besides this, Max told Irene that she had really let herself go with her weight, and he said it was obvious she wasn't interested in him sexually anymore. He thought that she should be thankful that he wasn't really cheating on her with another woman.

What are the possible causes of their problems, and how could they move forward?

Scenarios

Read 1 Cor. 7:2-5. What does St. Paul mean that the husband and wife should "fulfill their duties" to each other? What does he mean that they have authority over each other's bodies? Why should spouses not "deprive each other"?

11 Write out how you would like to react to the following, and how would you like your spouse to react:

- A miscarriage
- Death of a child
- Spouse losing a job
- Major personal illness
- Spouse undergoing a spiritual crisis
- A close friend makes a pass
- Finding yourself attracted to another person

5. Sex and Romance

Romance

The foundation of marriage is love. Love compels a man to leave his father and his mother in order to pursue his other half, his woman. He desires to become one with her, and she with him. This oneness has many dimensions. It usually begins with attraction and desire that is consummated in conjugal union on their wedding day. The Sacrament of Crowning is the establishing of a covenant of love between the man and woman that is sealed by a kiss in the service itself and by lovemaking in the marital bedchamber.

Love is designed to mature and grow. Eros runs ahead in the race at the beginning, but *philia* and *storge* are designed to outpace it in the long run. Finally, *agape* is to be the ultimate victor in the race to the Kingdom of God. Romance during courtship is central to mutual discovery and establishes a paradigm of intimacy that is to be developed and deepened over time. Sexual union is of great importance to young marriages and serves their oneness in many ways. As marriages mature, sex is designed to become more refined, less selfish, and ultimately less central to the union as the libido declines with age. By God's design, sexual desire decreases as the couple passes through earthly life, enabling the husband and wife to lift up their interests from the earth and to stretch out their hands and hearts towards heaven. Even as the role of sexual union changes, intimacy and romance are designed to continue and deepen. Marital love ought to become more and more unconditional over time, more uniquely sacrificial, and more secure as the couple deepens both their knowledge and trust in each other.

Sex

Sexuality is a profoundly important aspect of human existence and has great potential for both creation and for destruction. In secular culture, sex has been ripped out of its God-ordained context and has become animalistic, individualistic, selfish, and destructive. It is often associated not just with pleasure but with disease, violence, and death. A prime example is the way in which abortion is almost always used simply as a contraceptive method.

The Lord God designed sexual intercourse in this world to exist in a context of love, commitment, marriage, childbearing, and family rearing. Sex is never to be done simply for one's own pleasure. That is the sin of lust. Sex is always to be connected to love. It is to be an expression of a couple's singular devotion and rooted in commitment. A couple's commitment is to be connected to marriage as God has fashioned it: mysterious, complimentary, monogamous, unitive, indissoluble, and life-giving. This is the web of love that God has designed for human flourishing. This is the context in which sex has been fashioned by God. Embracing God's design for sex is the means by which it can become a powerful force for good. Rejecting God's design for sex is the means for misery in this life and the next. The Lord Jesus Christ said,

> "I have come that you might have life, and have it abundantly." [1]

Sexuality is such an important part of human life, and Jesus and His Church have much light to shine upon it.

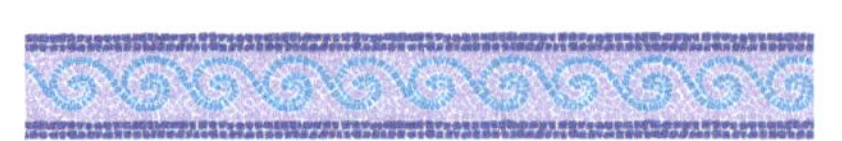

Sex in the Wedding Service

The Sacrament of Crowning is not shy about sex. Many prayers and petitions in the service directly refer to the sexual life of the couple.

First, the service presupposes that the couple are virgins. Premarital sex is not just an expression of lust, but an assault upon the institution of marriage itself. It is a plundering of the goods of marriage. It is a defiling of a holy thing. Only God has the right to join a couple into one flesh. The Church prays that God Himself would "crown the couple into one flesh." It is God's prerogative and His alone to crown into one flesh one of His sons to one of His daughters. A couple ought not to play God and crown themselves.

Faithful Christians look to a future at the Great Judgment seat when they hope to be crowned by Christ, and to join the innumerable multitude of saints who are adorned by crowns in heaven. Jesus counsels the Church in Philadelphia,

> "I am coming quickly; hold fast what you have, so that no one will take your crown." [2]

---

1   St. John 10:10
2   Rev. 3:11

The marriage crowns are God's gifts to the couple as a reward for their faithful struggle to be pure and present themselves as virgins to each other and before His priest on the wedding day. This is expressed liturgically in the Prayer for the Removing of the Crowns which is prayed when the newlyweds return from their honeymoon. In this prayer, the priest prays that the crowns have been granted to them as a "reward for continence":

> "O Lord our God, who hast blessed the crown of the year, and permittest these crowns to be laid upon those who are united to one another by the law of marriage, thereby granting unto them a reward for continence; for they are pure who are united in the marriage which thou hast made lawful: Do thou bless also in the removal of these crowns those who have been united to one another, and preserve their union indissoluble."

The crowns of marriage are the crowns of victors who have run the race of chastity unto marriage well. The white bridal dress is also designed as a witness to the purity of the bride. It is hypocrisy to wear the white of purity if the couple is sleeping together. The Bride comes to offer her virginity to her groom. The groom does the same. St. John Chrysostom says that the greatest and most important asset that a bride and groom can bring to their wedding day is not an education, real estate, or a career, but their own virginity. Nothing contributes to the happiness and stability of the

marriage more than this according to the Golden Mouth.

Decadent Western culture despises virginity, and openly mocks chastity. Therefore, many couples come to marriage severely wounded in their sexuality. It is important for these dear ones to remember that the grace of God triumphs over sin. St. Paul writes,

> "Where sin increased, grace abounded all the more."[3]

Couples that have lost their virginity can still obtain God's blessing and be crowned if they have repented of their sins.[4] Unmarried couples that are living together or have had sex should sincerely confess their sin to their father confessor and fulfill his counsel. Jesus is the most glorious and unusual Bridegroom. Earthly bridegrooms take the precious virginity of their brides, but the heavenly Bridegroom, our Lord Jesus Christ, actually embraces us in our defilement and His grace – given in Holy Baptism and subsequently in Holy Confession – restores our purity and resplendence through union with Him. Couples who have fallen ought to get up again and steady themselves in the commandments of God as they seek the blessing from God and the Church to wed. If the couple has been living together, they must by all means separate regardless of the difficulty in doing so if they hope to win God's forgiveness and blessing upon their marriage. Under

---

3 Romans 5:20
4 Only men who will be priests are required by the Church to marry virgins.

no circumstances ought a priest crown a couple while they are living together.

Prayers regarding the sexual relationship of the couple begin in the betrothal service itself. There, in the opening Litany of Peace, the celebrant intones,

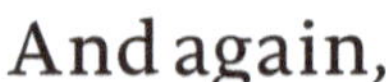

"That the Lord our God will grant unto them an honorable marriage, and a bed undefiled, let us pray to the Lord."

In the Great Betrothal Prayer, during which the couple places their rings upon each other's right hand, the celebrant prays,

"Establish them in the holy union which is from Thee. For Thou, in the beginning, didst make them male and female, and by thee is the woman joined unto the man as a helpmate and for the procreation of the human race."

In the first Crowning Prayer we pray,

"Bless this marriage and grant to these Thy servants...chastity." [5]

And again,

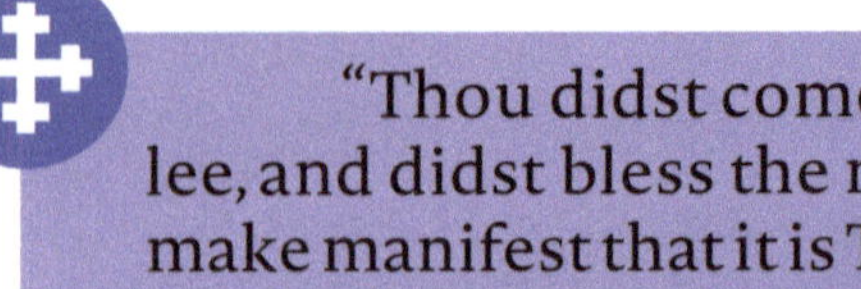

"Thou didst come to Cana of Galilee, and didst bless the marriage there, to make manifest that it is Thy will that there should be lawful marriage and procreation."

Lawful marriage, lawful procreation, marital chastity – these are simply God's will. God wants marriage and procreation. The prayer continues,

"Preserve their bed un-assailed."

In the second Crowning Prayer we pray,

"Grant them of the fruit of their bodies fair children, and concord of soul and body."

In the third Crowning Prayer we pray,

"Wed them into one flesh."

In the prayer at the end of the Litany of Supplication following the Crowning Prayers, we pray these words for the newly united couple:

5   There are different degrees of chastity in the Church. Monks and nuns who consecrated their virginity to God practice "angelic chastity." Husband and wives who conduct their sexual relations according to God's will with dignity practice "marital chastity" which is what this prayer is asking God to grant the couple.

"O Lord our God, Who in Thy saving providence didst vouchsafe by Thy presence in Cana of Galilee to declare marriage honorable: Do thou, the same Lord, now also maintain in peace and concord Thy servants, N. and N., whom Thou hast been pleased to join together. Cause their marriage to be honorable. Preserve their bed blameless. Mercifully grant that they may live together in purity, even unto a ripe old age, walking in Thy commandments with a pure heart."

Here we directly pray God's blessing down upon the couple's marriage bed. We pray that what goes on there would be blameless. We pray that they may live in purity together until they are very old.

God's Purposes for Sex in Marriage

According to the Holy Scriptures and the teachings of the Church Fathers, there are three God-ordained purposes for sexual intercourse in marriage. These purposes are:

· To tame the wild nature of men and women and heal their disordered passions, thus assisting on the path of *theosis*.

· To procreate children, which is a mighty miracle, and thus contribute to the upbuilding of the Church, family, and state.

· To serve as a powerful adhesive between husband and wife, a sort of nuptial glue promoting marital harmony and unity.

The Purpose of Sexual Union to Tame Man

St. Paul the Apostle teaches us that sexual union in marriage is the primary way that men and women overcome the virus of lust. It is the death knell of sexual immorality. The apostle writes,

"Because of immoralities, let each man have his own wife, and let each woman have her own husband. Let the husband fulfill his duty to his wife, and likewise also the wife to her husband. The wife does not have authority over her own body, but the husband does; and likewise also the husband does not have authority over his own body, but the wife does. Stop depriving one another, except by agreement for a time that you may devote yourselves to prayer, and come together again lest Satan tempt you because of your lack of self-control."[6]

Since our fall from grace, our passions have been disordered. For most people, this disorder is particularly noticeable in powerful sexual drives.

Sexual relations in marriage provide a safe and calm harbor to tame and redirect these unruly passions and desires. Christian marriage, and the God-blessed sexual union which attends this mystery of the Church, is the antidote to sexual immorality and the tyranny of lust. The revered early church theologian and catechist, Clement of Alexandria, calls marriage a "disciplined pleasure."[7] Conjugal union provides for certain natural needs. God has given the married each other to serve as a calming drug, as a love charm, and as a calm harbor in a very stormy sexual sea. By adhering to the Church's inspired sexual guidance, and by confining their sexual desire, thoughts, and actions to their spouse, a couple tames the beast and forces sexual energy into its lawful outlet.

The Purpose of Sexual Union to Procreate
Not only does marital intercourse work to refine and tame fallen human passions, but God has also given to it a life-giving and creative power. The Church Fathers teach us that the Lord God attached great pleasure to sexual union in order to encourage man to procreate. The challenges of birth-giving and raising a family are such that, if sexual union was not such an intense pleasure, many men and women might have avoided having children and have remained locked in their selfish existences until death. Through the pleasure of physical union of man and woman, God has ordained that the human race should increase, that His image should be multiplied, and that the Church should be built up. The commandment first given to Adam and Eve was this:

> "Be fruitful and multiply, fill the earth, and subdue it, and rule."[8]

After the Fall, this commandment has been fulfilled through sexual union in marriage. The commandment has relevance also for monastics, who are called upon to multiply godly thoughts and deeds, and for the Church as a whole to multiply spiritual children. But the commandment continues in procreative force for married couples. Marital sex is not something apart from the commandments of God or detached from one's religious commitments. It is the means towards fulfilling one of the most sacred obligations of married couples.

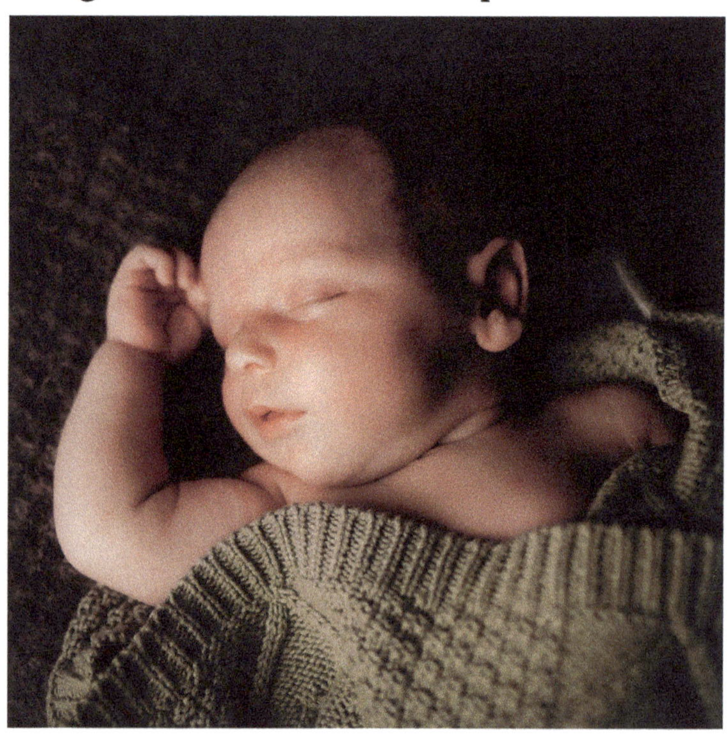

---

7   Stromate III, Ferguson (1991), p. 297.

8   Genesis 1:28

The Purpose of Sexual Union to Promote Marital Union and Harmony

Commenting upon Proverbs 5:18-19, St. Gregory the Theologian describes conjugal union as a "seal of natural affection." He writes,

"For man and wife the union of wedlock is a bolted door securing chastity and restraining desire. And it is a seal of natural affection. They possess the loving colt which cheers the heart by gamboling, and a single drink from their private fountain untasted by strangers, which neither flows outwards, nor gathers its waters from without. Wholly united in the flesh, concordant in spirit, by love they sharpen in one another a like spur to piety."

In the words of the esteemed Athonite elder, Hieromonk Gregorios of Dionysiou,

"Sexual relations were given as succor for strengthening the loving relationship of the couple and helping them to face the struggles of family life."[9]

For married Christians, the sensual meadows walked through in conjugal union are designed to seal their affection, and to nurture mutual respect, kindness, affection, and loyalty. Many annoyances are quickly buried through marital union, and this is a blessing for harmony. Marital union also serves to prevent estrangement and alienation. It is rare for sexual union not to be preceded by some level of intimate communication, and that strengthens the marriage bond. The union of intercourse is to be a type of the union of souls between the partners. Sexual intercourse is designed as marital glue. Many husbands, for instance, are motivated by their desire for their wives to act with more sincere consideration and a more tender communication. Becoming one flesh should have a powerful psychological effect on the couple and cement their exclusivity. They belong to each other in a way no one else does, and they are meant to stay bound.

Marital Chastity

St. John Chrysostom writes,

"Desire is not sin: but when it has run into extravagance, being not minded to keep within the laws of marriage, but springing even upon other men's wives."

Clement of Alexandria says that

"Lust is desire disobedient to reason."

It is lust, not desire, that is sinful. St. Paul's dictum, "Be angry, but do not sin" may be applied to the passion of sexual desire thus: "Desire your wife, but do not sin." St. John of Damascus says that such natural but unnecessary pleasures as marital intercourse ought to be enjoyed in fitting season, manner, and measure.[10] St. Photios the Great says that

---

9   The Mystery of Marriage: A Fellowship of Love (2013), Newrome Press, p. 24.

10   Exposition of the Orthodox Faith, II, 13, translated by Frederic H. Chase, Jr. (1958), Catholic University of America Press: Washington D.C., p. 240. The great Father goes on to say that "Such pleasures may be considered to be good as do not involve pain, cause remorse, do any damage, exceed the limits of moderation, distract us for long from good works, or enslave us."

sexual pleasure in marriage is lawful.[11] St. Gregory Palamas speaks of marriage as God's gift and love-making as permissible pleasure to be exercised chastely.[12] The Church Fathers preach dignified sexuality. The West's contemporary obsession with sex is debased and non-Christian, but this does not nullify the legitimacy of chaste conjugal love. Father Seraphim Rose writes,

"In the 'free world' a great exploitative force is that of 'sex.' It seems to be today a vast, impersonal power that holds men in its jaws, leading them on not only to reproduce their kind but – thanks to the many devices for 'exploiting' this power more efficiently – to indulge this impersonal force for its own sake. Some may object that 'sex' is indeed a very 'personal' thing, but nothing could be further from the truth. Like all other human impulses, the sexual instinct may be subordinated to the power of personality and attain its proper place as an expression of married, chaste love; but only the most naïve romanticist could affirm that such is the 'sex' that is exalted today. Sex as pleasure, as an expression of man's freedom to do what he pleases: this is what it means to contemporary man."[13]

Christians will always believe in the chastity of marriage. In fact, the word chastity is used throughout the wedding service. In the opening Great Litany of the Crowning Service the celebrant intones, "That He will give them chastity, and of the fruit of the womb as is expedient for them, let us pray to the Lord." Some may wonder why we are praying for the couple to have chastity when they are getting married and looking forward to sleeping together. This is because there are different kinds of chastity, and there is a particular form of chastity called "marital chastity."

The highest form of chastity, exhibited by our Lord Jesus Christ, by His Mother the Most Pure Theotokos, by the Holy Prophet and Forerunner John the Baptist, and by many monks and nuns throughout Christian history is angelic chastity. It is, according to St. Athanasius the Great, a chastity that is angelic and unsurpassed, and is embraced by those who are called to the angelic estate of monasticism. There is another dignified form of chastity for those who are called to holy matrimony. This is virginal chastity prior to marriage, and marital chastity after being crowned. Marital chastity is more moderate and ordinary according to St. Athanasius, but it has its own boast. Married couples are called to express their sexuality in chaste ways.

Marital chastity has both a positive and a negative dimension. Positively, married couples are called to channel their sexual desire in the ways of love, to literally "make love", that is, to have sex as an expression of tender intimacy, deep respect, a communication of love, a mutual delight, a means of pleasing the other, and according to nature

---

11   Homily on the Birth of the Virgin, 9, in Cyril Mango (1958) The Homilies of Photius, Patriarch of Constantinople, Cambridge, MA :Harvard University Press, p. 174.

12   Homily 5, On the Meeting of the Lord, translated by Christopher Veniamin (2009), Waymart, PA: Mt. Thabor Publishing.

13   Hieromonk Damascene (2003) Father Seraphim Rose: His Life and Works, St. Herman of Alaska Press: Platina, Ca., p. 151

and the Law of God. Negatively, married couples are called to check their sexual desire from selfishness, lust, animalistic practices, insensitivity, and perversion. Marital chastity requires the couples to maintain God's blessing upon their union by not thinking perverted thoughts, not over-indulging, and not practicing unnatural sexual acts.

Marriage is not a legal cover for perversion. Sexual perversion outside of marriage is the same as sexual perversion within marriage. Marriage does not make the unnatural natural. In the contemporary secular West, we live in a culture of sexual anarchy where natural and moral norms for sexual behavior have been all but completely abandoned. We must learn again from our Holy Mother Church the norms of dignified sexuality. As you work through the rest of this chapter and we discuss intimate matters, I suggest that you simply blush once, get this out of the way, and then educate yourself. The Holy Scriptures and the Holy Fathers would not have dedicated so much inspired instruction to sex and marital chastity if it were not important to our salvation and the dignity of our marriages.

Forms of Unnatural Sexuality to Be Avoided

When St. Paul wrote his words to the Hebrews, charging them to honor marriage and preserve the marriage bed undefiled, it was *adultery* that was foremost in his mind as the defiler of the sanctity of the marriage bed. Christian men and women are called by the Lord God in marriage to be *sexually content* with their one and only spouse. The Proverbs of Solomon offer the following sexual advice,

> "Drink water from your own cistern, flowing water from your own well. Should your springs be scattered abroad, streams of water in the streets? Let them be for yourself alone, and not for strangers with you. Let your fountain be blessed, and rejoice in the wife of your youth, a lovely hind, a graceful doe. Let her breasts satisfy you at all times, be infatuated always with her love. Why should you be infatuated, my son, with a loose woman and embrace the bosom of an adulteress? For a man's ways are before the eyes of the Lord."[14]

Violations of the seventh commandment – "thou shalt not commit adultery" – are quite prevalent today. According to reliable statistical studies, between

25%-33% of married men admit to having at least one extramarital affair. The stats for women are slightly lower at 17%-25%.[15] Any way one looks at it, the occurrence of marital infidelity is staggering.

Besides adulterous affairs, there are many other common forms of adultery. The statistics quoted above do not reflect the Christian understanding of illegitimate divorce and remarriage as constituting a form of adultery. Jesus clearly taught all divorce and remarriage, except for the cause of unchastity, is adulterous,

> "Whoever divorces his wife makes her commit adultery, and whoever marries a divorced woman commits adultery."[16]

From the perspective of Christianity then, the occurrence of adultery in our culture is significantly higher than the statistics above would lead us to believe. Whenever a couple divorces for unjustifiable reasons and then remarries, they have committed adultery. Many persons may very well only discover on the great Day of Judgment that their divorces and multiple marriages were adulterous. Prostitution is also a common form of adultery. Besides affairs, illicit divorce, and the use of prostitutes and other "hook-ups", new forms of adultery have arisen in today's world associated with bio-medical technology such as surrogate motherhood, artificial insemination, and in-vitro fertilization. These technologies insert third parties (doctors and surrogates) into the intimate union of husband and wife and their exclusive pro-creative acts.

Marital chastity is defiled not just by adultery, but by unnatural sexual activity within marriage. These unnatural acts include *oral sex* which is castigated by the Church as a wasteful discharge of semen, a useless expenditure, and a custom not in harmony with nature. A man's semen is holy, and to seek orgasm without intercourse is to act against nature. The husband's seed is designed by God to be discharged into the field of the wife's uterus. We find oral sex explicitly forbidden in the writings of the Church Fathers, where it is styled the "iniquity of the mouth."[17] Other unnatural sex acts include *anal sex*, the commission of which by a husband with his wife makes the Christian husband worse than any homosexual according to the Church Fathers. Lastly, masturbation, pornography use, and the refusal of sex's life-creating potentiality by the use of artificial contraception are considered by the Church to be a defilement of the marriage bed.

When a Spouse's Demands Are Sinful and Should Be Refused

Many men today, even Christian men deeply damaged by internet pornography, expect their wives to satisfy

---

15   Samuel Janus and Cynthia Janus (1993), The Janus Report on Sexual Behavior, New York: John Wiley and Sons, p. 169. These statistics have held steady for the last three decades. For more see the work of Professor Nicholas Wolfinger at the University of Utah.

16   St. Mark 10:.

17   Letter to Barnabas, 10.8 as quoted in John T. Noonan (1965), Contraception: A History of Its Treatment by the Catholic Theologians and Canonists, Cambridge, MA: Harvard University Press, p. 92.

their every perverse desire. Priests are constantly confronted by pastoral situations in which wives are afraid because their husbands are demanding them to participate in ungodly sexual acts. Should a wife accommodate her husband in such a situation? The answer must be a firm "no." A woman must not exalt her husband's requests above the commands of God. She serves God before she serves her husband, and the service to the husband must be a service to, and in, God.

At the same time, a wife should not use the Church as a cover to escape her legitimate conjugal duties or to hurt her husband's feelings. Sometimes a woman, who is less interested in sex or possibly bored by it, uses the Church as a tool to put off her husband. Such behavior is unloving and sinful. Some husbands will interpret a wife's refusal to perform an impermissible sex act as a personal rejection, especially if the couple has practiced this in their personal history. In such cases, the wife should humbly explain her concern in a context in which she affirms her desire for her husband and her sincere wish to please him sexually. The husband must remember that he is not God, and he does not "own" his wife. She is his God-given partner in a sacred union designed for their salvation. If a husband is going to make a fuss about not getting sex acts which are not blessed, he must know that he is a lover of the flesh and that Jesus is expecting him to repent. Husbands will be judged for such things on the dread Day of Judgment. Loving husbands lead their wives in marital intimacy that is upright.

Discussion Questions

1 From whom did you learn the basic facts of sex? How might your opinions about sex be impacted by those from whom you learned?

2 How do you think a couple's Christian faith would most impact their sexual life?

3 How might a couple practically develop a more loving and less selfish sexual life?

4 You recently visited a monastery, and had a conversation with a monk that left you feeling that sex, even in marriage, was probably dirty and that it would be best to avoid it. What should you do with these thoughts?

5 What practical steps might you as a couple take to nourish God's purposes for your sex life?
- To tame your disordered passions?
- To have children and build up the Church?
- To nourish marital harmony and unity?

6 What practical steps might you as a couple take to nourish your marital chastity?

Exercises

Scenarios of Intimacy Issue Resolution

1 After the birth of a couple's first child, the spouses begin to experience a feeling of lost intimacy. The husband begins to interpret his wife's commitment to motherhood as though he is being replaced as her top priority. The wife finds herself exhausted, and finds the couple's past path to intimacy hard to attain.

How might the couple forge a new path for sexual intimacy and closeness?

2 After twenty years of contented sexual life, your spouse begins to feel unsatisfied with your sexual life. The discontented spouse asks you if the two of you could experiment with some sexual practices that you both have always considered unnatural.

What should you do?

(Continued on the next page)

Exercises

Scenarios of Intimacy Issue Resolution

3 After forty years of marriage, it is revealed to you that your spouse has been having an illicit affair for some years with a close family friend.

How would you want to respond?

4 As the couple prepares to celebrate their 30th anniversary, the husband begins to experience erectile dysfunction (ED) as is common for men as they approach 60. This health challenge is negatively impacting the husband's sense of wholeness and manliness.

What might the husband do?

What might the wife do?

6. Children and Parenting

We taught in our last chapter that one of the central purposes of sex in marriage is procreation. The first words God uttered into the ears of the first married couple, Adam and Eve, were the words: "Be fruitful and multiply." The life-giving nature of marriage can be no more tinkered with than can the callings of sacred companionship and sexual chastity. Marriage is not a wax nose to be played with. Marriage is a package deal. As a priest I have the honor of conducting premarital counseling with couples who intend to be wed in the Church. Usually in our very first meeting I ask the couple individually if they are really prepared to embrace marriage. I remind them that marriage is designed by God to be a sacred companionship, an exclusive sexually faithful conjugal union, and life-giving love through which children are fashioned.

Then I ask each of the persons this:

Are you ready to be a faithful companion all your life? Are you ready to be the best friend and chief companion of the other without allowing anyone else on earth to take that place? If either the young man or the young woman is not yet ready to be each other's chief partner and friend, then I ask them to come back to me when they are ready since this is a *non-negotiable* aspect of marriage. If they are ready to be each other's companion, we move on to question #2: Are you ready to be sexually faithful to your spouse alone all your life? Are you ready to eschew every other sexual partner for as long as you live? If the answer is no, and either one or both are not able to bring themselves to commit to monogamy, I ask the couple to come back to me when they are ready to do so because this is a *non-negotiable* aspect of marriage. If they are ready to be each other's faithful sexual partner for their whole lives, we move on to question #3: Are you ready to have children following your marriage? Are you ready to embrace the life-giving nature of the marriage union? Often at this moment someone will say that he or she is ready for children but just "not yet." Often I hear from the couple, "Well we would like to live together for four or five years before we have children." Because procreation is just as fundamental to marriage as sexual fidelity, this statement is just as ridiculous as saying, "We would like to be free to have sex with others for the first four or five years of our marriage before we settle down to sexual fidelity," or "We would like to keep our other friends and buddies in their same place in our lives for the next four or five years of our marriage before we become each other's top priority." To intentionally put off procreation for four or five years after marriage is to treat procreation as a *non-essential* aspect of marriage, as though it is something the married couple is free to take or leave. That is simply not true. If a couple is not ready to be open to the gift of children following marital love-making, then the couple is not ready for marriage itself; marriage is a "package deal" and cannot be "cut-up" into pieces by the couple so they can take the parts they want and leave aside the parts they don't. If you are not ready for the package, don't open it.

The Overwhelming Emphasis on Procreation in the Wedding Service Itself

The first time that the names of the couple are mentioned in the wedding service is during the opening litany of the betrothal in which the clergy and people gathered pray for the couple's salvation. That petition is immediately followed by a petition for the blessed procreation of the couple,

"That they may be granted children for the continuation of the race, and all their petitions which are unto salvation, let us pray to the Lord."

Note that as soon as we begin to pray specifically for the couple we pray for their salvation in marriage, and as soon as we pray for their salvation in marriage we pray for them to have children because *learning to love and care for children is the path of salvation for married couples.* It is exactly here in the narrow path of parenting where a husband and wife learn to die together to their selfish ambitions and to live for and serve their children.

By the prominence of this petition the Church is also forthright not only to point out how fundamental child-bearing is to marriage and how honorable it is, but also how important it is to the entire Church and to the entire human race. The sexual revolution of the 1960s trivialized sex as a private matter, but the Church has always viewed sexuality as matter of *grave ecclesial and public consequence.* This is why the Church has *always* cared about what goes on or doesn't go on in a couple's bedroom. Sexuality is an incredibly important aspect of human life, and as such the light of the Lord cannot be absent from the bedrooms of the faithful. We pray that the couple may be granted children "for the continuation of the race." The whole Christian race and indeed even the entire human race depends on faithful child-bearing. When couples do not accept the responsibility from God to bear and raise children, as is the case in the contemporary West since the 1960s, entire cultures fall into demographic winter, decline, and die. This is one of the central reasons that the Orthodox Church is shrinking in the West. More Orthodox Christians have been catechized by the sexual revolution than by the Christian faith, and the consequence is that Orthodox families have dwindled and the population of believers has radically declined.[1]

For a Helpmate and the Procreation of the Human Race

The service continues with the Great Prayer of Betrothal during which the celebrant ponders on how God providentially arranges marriages as He did that of Isaac and Rebecca. The priest continues by asking God to establish the

couple in a "holy union" so that by God's agency the woman might become a

"helpmate and for the procreation of the human race."

Every Christian marriage has the future of the human race in its hands.

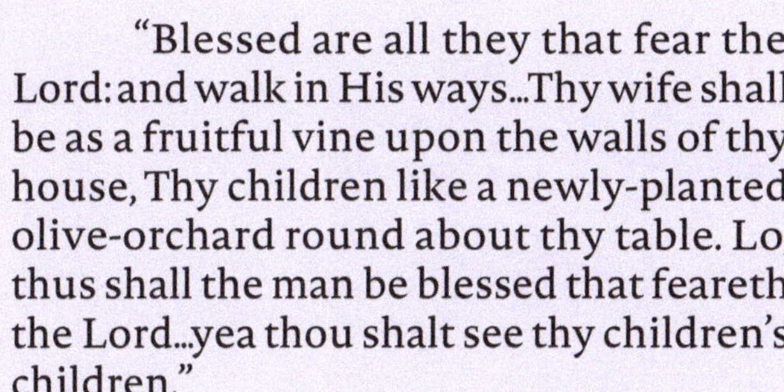

Wife as a Fruitful Vine

The Crowning Service begins with the chanting of the wedding psalms 126 and 127. These are the first words heard in the wedding service proper:

> "Blessed are all they that fear the Lord: and walk in His ways…Thy wife shall be as a fruitful vine upon the walls of thy house, Thy children like a newly-planted olive-orchard round about thy table. Lo, thus shall the man be blessed that feareth the Lord…yea thou shalt see thy children's children."

This Psalm together with Psalm 126 hymn the glory of children as a special blessing, gift and reward from God to the couple. Psalm 126:1-5a reads,

> "Unless the Lord builds the house, they labor in vain who build it; unless the Lord guards the city, the watchman keeps awake in vain. It is vain for you to rise up early, to retire late, to eat the bread of painful labors; For he gives to His beloved even in sleep. Behold, children are a gift of the Lord; the fruit of the womb is a reward. Like arrows in the hand of a warrior, so are the children of one's youth. How blessed is the man whose quiver is full of them."

---

1   The same is true for Roman Catholic and Protestant families.

This is the Scriptural perspective on the preciousness of having children. Embracing this conviction is one of the greatest contradictions of the unbelieving and secular culture that a Christian couple can make. Indeed, the gift of children is one of God's highest and most precious gifts, and yet so many people are studiously resolved to avoid it!

"Sons and Daughters"

These are the exact words we use in our petition to God for the couple in the Crowning Service:

> "that God will make them glad with the sight of sons and daughters, let us pray to the Lord."

Notice the plurals. You don't have to be a mathematician to know that the fulfillment of these prayers in general takes the bearing of at least four children! The very next petition continues the theme of children,

> "That He will grant them enjoyment in the blessing of children, and a blameless life, let us pray to the Lord."

Fruit of the Womb as is Expedient

Many Christians today worry greatly about how many children they should have, as though this is something that the couple should primarily decide themselves, instead of trusting God's providence in this important matter. The text of the opening Great Litany places the emphasis on family size elsewhere,

> "That He will give them chastity, and of the fruit of the womb as is expedient for them."

We pray in the service that God will tailor the procreation of the soon-to-be married couple to their good. We ask Him to give them the number of children that is "expedient" for them. God knows best. He knows what is expedient for us. We can trust Him with the decision of how many children we ought to have, just as we will trust Him with each and every day of the lives of the children He does give us.

Be Fruitful and Multiply

In the first Crowning Prayer the priest recites the first words that God spoke to the couple,

> "Be fruitful and multiply, and fill the earth."

Then the priest recites how God blessed Abraham and Sarah with children, and Isaac and Rebecca – whose childbearing God blessed. God joined Jacob and Rachel and from them brought forth the twelve patriarchs. God united Joseph and Asenath and blessed them with Ephraim and Manasseh. God gave St. John the Baptist to Zacharias and Elizabeth. Christ came to Cana to show forth that there should be lawful marriage and procreation. The priest prays that God would grant to the couple "long-lived offspring" and "gratitude from their children."

Offspring like Full Ears of Grain

In the second Crowning Prayer the priest prays,

"Grant them the fruit of their bodies fair children, and concord of soul and body; exalt them like the cedars of Lebanon, like a luxuriant vine. Give them offspring in number like full ears of grain; so that having sufficiency in all things, they may abound in every work that is good."

Here the number of children is actually prayed for. What is that number? Full ears of grain, that is, wheat and barley grains. If you look at a wheat stalk you will find on one stem between 10 and 20 ears. How's that for being fruitful and multiplying? And note how many children are connected to the couple's confidence in having sufficiency, in suffering no want or lack in anything, and in being able to abound in good deeds.

The third Crowning Prayer also asks God to grant the couple

"the fruit of the body and procreation of fair children."

All three Crowning Prayers – the very center of the wedding service – focus upon procreation and child-bearing. The core of these central prayers is having and raising children.

Multiply like Jacob and Rachel

At the conclusion of the Crowning Service, the celebrant removes the crowns and the priest blesses both the Bridegroom and the Bride individually with these words,

"Be thou exalted, O bridegroom, like unto Abraham; and be thou blessed, like unto Isaac, and do thou multiply like unto Jacob, walking in peace, and keeping the commandments of God in righteousness."

And then the priest blesses the Bride saying,

"And thou, O Bride: Be thou exalted like unto Sarah; and exult thou like unto Rebecca; and do thou multiply unto Rachel; and rejoice thou in thy husband, fulfilling the conditions of the law: for so it is well-pleasing unto God."

In these beautiful blessings the priest blessed the couple to have twelve children like Jacob and Rachel!

The Final Nuptial Blessing

The last blessing of the wedding service is made by the celebrant with the hand-cross over the newly-crowned couple. He again asks the blessing of the All-Holy, Consubstantial, and Life-Giving Trinity to bless the couple with length of days, fair children, and prosperity of life. The blessing of children simply permeates the entire wedding service from beginning to end, and the Church trusts that the Lord will provide a corresponding "prosperity of life" with the children that God gives to the couple.

St. John Chrysostom, reflecting upon procreation in marriage, calls it

"sweet and universally desirable."

This is the Christian mind, but it is far from the secular mind. In secular society children are viewed as burdens, and despised. Contraception is called "protection" as though children are dangerous monsters that husbands and wives need to be protected from. On the contrary, parents don't need to be saved from children: parents need to be saved *by* children. The bearing and rearing of children is the narrow path through which those called by God to marriage work out their own salvation with fear and trembling. The real monsters from which the couple needs protection are not their future children, but their egos, self-centeredness, and self-love. Children and parenting are the means of protecting couples from these monsters. The newly-glorified

St. Sophrony of Essex puts it this way in his well-known word on marriage:

"The purpose of Christian marriage is for people to reach unselfish love and cut off their own will, and thence to reach God."

The Christian Vision of Procreation

It is obvious from the superabundance of references to procreation that the Church sets forth a profound vision for human reproduction in marriage. This glorious perspective flows from two deep convictions of the Church. The first conviction is that the destiny of the world is to be full of the glory of God. This is the witness of the prophets like Habakkuk who wrote,

"For the earth will be filled with the knowledge of the glory of the Lord, as the waters cover the sea."[2]

The second conviction is that human beings are the means of filling the earth with God's glory. The Holy Fathers teach that a single human person is more valuable to God than is the entire created cosmos. Human beings are uniquely fashioned in the image of God and manifest His glory. As such, we are God's agents for covering the entire earth with the knowledge of God.

St. Ambrose of Milan teaches that there are two fundamental ways that believers fulfill the Great Commission to make disciples of all the nations. One

---

is to preach the Gospel to unbelievers and to baptize them. The second is for devout Christian families to have children and raise them to love God. And of the two, the latter is the most effective. Accepting the responsibility of procreation in marriage is not just essential for the salvation of the couple and the continuance of the human race, but it is also essential for the fulfillment of the missionary calling of the Church. The Great Commission depends on it.

Moses and Pharaoh

The world has always had difficulty understanding the Christian conviction about the preciousness of human beings. This is the way it was when Moses was alive. The Egyptians did not believe that all human beings are precious, being made in the image of God. They believed such things about *themselves*, but thought that the Israelites were completely different. Pharaoh asserted that the Israelites were born to be slaves, and some of them were not designed to be born at all! This is why Pharaoh sought to kill all the male Israelite children. When Moses penned the book of Genesis and opened his first chapter with an affirmation of the equality of all human beings as created in the image of God, this was a most radical notion that struck at the very heart of the Egyptian worldview, just as it continues to strike at all similarly deficient worldviews – like those of the Hindus with their caste system, the Chinese with their one-child policy, and the modern Western-Secularists with their dehumanization of the unborn child through abortion or the elderly and infirmed through euthanasia. In the face of all such human degradation, we Christians affirm that one human being is worth more to God than the entire creation. Every one of your children is that valuable, so who would not want to have children? *Only those who do not really believe this about the human being, or are confused and fearful or overwhelmed at the thought of parenthood.*

In Moses' day, kings expressed and affirmed their rule over their kingdoms by placing their images in city squares throughout their territory. Travel was difficult, and there was no television or internet to broadcast a presidential address to the living rooms of the citizens of the kingdom. Instead, the imperial images were set up throughout the kingdom and the citizens related to the images as they would relate directly to the king. They would make their bows before the regal image, and their obeisance was accepted by the king as obeisance to him directly. Of course, it worked the opposite way also. Any dishonor done to the imperial image was a direct offense to the king and punishable with death. It is with this background in mind that we should hear the Scriptural teaching about man being made in the image of God. Human beings were created as the glory of God, and to express His rule and sovereignty over all of creation by their very being. Man represents God on the earth. This is how special human beings are, and how central to God's eternal plan.

The Mystery of Procreation

When a couple conceives and bears a child, they are functioning as *co-creators* with God of infinitely valuable persons who will live forever. We do not really reproduce like animals, despite the surface-level similarities. Human procreation is far more than a merely biological reality: it is an immensely beautiful, profound, dignified, personal, and mysterious process. Each and every conception and birth is a miracle of creation *ex nihilo*.[3] Listen also to St. Methodios of Olympus hymn the beauty of procreation:

"Man's coming into existence begins with the sowing of seed in the furrows of the maternal field: and thus bone from bone and flesh from flesh, taken in an invisible act of power and always by the same divine Craftsman, are fashioned into a human being...that first sleep of Adam was to be a type of man's enchantment in love, when in his thirst for children he falls into a trance, lulled to sleep by the pleasures of procreation, in order that a new person might be formed...for under the stimulation of intercourse, the body's harmony – so we are told by those who have consummated the rites of marriage – is greatly disturbed, and all the marrow-like generative part of the blood...rushes through the generative organs into the living soil of the woman...for man made one with woman in the embrace of love is overcome by a desire for children and completely forgets everything else...he offers his rib to his divine Creator, to be removed that he himself the father may appear once again in a son."

Sexual intercourse in Christian marriage is intended to be an *invisible act of power* in which the husband and wife, in the embrace of love, mystically cooperate with God, the divine Craftsman, in the creation of another human being. The desire for children is sublime, and this desire is born of a deep conviction that nothing is as precious in the universe

---

3   The Lord God fashions the human body out of the offering of sperm and egg from the parents, but the human soul is fashioned by the hand of God from nothing.

as a human being. Remember, this deep appreciation of marriage and procreation is coming from the pen of one of the greatest proponents of virginity and monastic life in the history of the Church, St. Methodios of Olympus.

No one describes the glory of procreation more intimately and beautifully than St. John Chrysostom in his twelfth homily on Colossians. There he writes:

"They come together, and the two make one...making an image of God Himself...they come about to be made one body. See again a mystery of love. If the two become not one, so long as they continue two, they make not many, but when they are come into oneness, they then make many. What do we learn from this? That great is the power of union. The wise counsel of God at the beginning divided the one into two; and being desirous of showing that even after the division it remaineth still one, He suffered not that the one should be of itself enough for procreation... Seest thou the mystery of marriage? He made of one, one; and again, having made these two, one, He so maketh one, so that now also man is produced of one. For man and wife are not two men, but one Man... They are two halves...a father rejoiceth both when son and daughter marry, as though the body were hastening to join a member of its own...each one separately is imperfect for the procreation of children, each one is imperfect as regards the constitution of this present life...And how become they one flesh? As if thou shouldest take away the purest part of gold, and mingle it with other gold; so in truth here also the woman as it were receiving the richest part fused by pleasure, nourisheth it and cherisheth it, and withal contributing her own share,

restoreth it back a Man. And the child is a sort of bridge, so that the three become one flesh, the child connecting, on either side, each to the other. For like as two cities, which a river divides throughout, become one, if a bridge connect them on both sides, so is it in this case...Nay, for their coming together hath this effect, it diffuses and commingles the bodies of both. And as one hath cast ointment in oil, hath made the whole one; so in truth is it also here."

A Vision for Parenting

The raising of children is the "most holy of all holy works," says St. Theophan the Recluse.[4] This is true because parenting is the raising of the image of God. It is the formation of God's children, a sacred task that God Himself has delegated to parents. Parents are stewards of the children that God has given them. It is the greatest honor for a mother and father to raise children, and because it is of such

---

4 Raising Them Right (1989), Mt. Hermon, Ca.: Conciliar Press, pp. 83-84.

seriousness and incredible value it is the hardest thing in the world. Parenting will either strengthen a marriage union past all expectations or it will blow it to smithereens.

The Scriptures themselves are overflowing with both didactic instruction for parenting, and moving narratives concerning parenting. The Proverbs of Solomon are replete with wisdom for family life. Think of Adam and Eve with their children Cain, Abel, and Seth. Think of Noah with his children, Shem, Ham and Japheth. Think of Abraham and his children, Moses and Zipporah and their children, King David and his children, the Much-Suffering Prophet Job and his children. The Biblical narratives are full of profound instruction for parents. The Patristic Tradition is also rich in teaching for parents. One of the most famous treatises on parenting is from St. John Chrysostom and is entitled *On Vainglory and the Proper Upbringing of Children.*

This treatise begins with a reflection upon values, since values guide the parenting praxis. Amongst the fundamental values that the Golden Mouth emphasizes is that parenting for the couple is a matter of their own salvation. Child-rearing is a transformative process not only for the children but for the parents. The Lord God forms the children through the instruction of the parents, and He forms the parents through the difficulties and challenges of parenting. Both parents and children are actively being parented by God Himself. This is a very important reality. The birth of a first child is a catapult toward maturity. Each new child is a new calling from God in our own spiritual maturation. No couple should parent as though they have "arrived." We are all works in process, and this spirit of mutual learning can greatly lubricate the inevitable shoulder-rubbing that is part and parcel of parenting.

As parents our goal is not always to be giving orders or directions to be obeyed by our children. While teaching obedience is greatly important, especially on matters of faith and safety, often we can teach obedience by being obedient ourselves to the will and desires of our spouse and the children. By choosing to deny his own wants and to acquiesce to the choices of his children concerning the simple matters of what is for dinner, what is for recreation this evening, and so on, the father provides a powerful witness to self-denial and love that will encourage mature obedience in the children. Parents can show their children the necessity of cutting off their own selfish wills *by example.*

Other principles articulated by St. John are that parents – not tutors, the state, or the church – are responsible before God for their children. He also sets forth parenting as an art where the parents are working on human masterpieces. As such parenting is a daily, often an hourly, investment of incrementally nourishing virtues and erasing vices.

The ultimate goal in parenting is to raise up athletes for Christ. In the wedding service the bride and groom are crowned as King and Queen of their own family. As such they are responsible for the domain which is their common family life and home. They must draw up both their own law codes and their own methods of enforcement. All of the focus of the home-kingdom ought be upon the development of Christian love and virtue. The parents must seek to fashion their home as a domestic church in which their own unique home typikon is enshrined. The parents seek to sanctify the senses of the child and to provide them with a Christian education such that their sons and daughters learn to worship and serve God and take up their positions as members of the Body of Christ. Toward that end, parents should make sure that their children know their bishop and spiritual father personally.

Practical Advice for Parenting

Parenting, like marriage itself, ought to be nourished, studied, and developed so it can mature over time. Parents ought to be always learning to be better parents, trying experiments, rejoicing, and repenting.

The greatest gift parents can give to their children is the parents' own inner life with God. Children learn above all else by observation and imitation. If we want our children to love, we must love. If we want our children to pray and serve God, we must pray and serve God. If we want our children to embrace responsibility with joy, we must embrace responsibility with joy. If our walk does not authentically express our talk, then our talk will be in vain. Each child has two ears and two eyes. They listen to what we say and they see what we do. We cannot guard the senses of our children if we ourselves are not well-guarded. We cannot infuse beauty, truth and goodness into our children if we are not cultivating beauty, truth and goodness in ourselves. St. Chrysostom encourages parents that they can make up for their own youthful misadventures and sinful failings by dedicating themselves to parenting. There is no reason that our children need to replicate our stupidity.

The second greatest gift parents can give to their children is another brother or sister. Growing up in a home with the support and friendship of brothers and sisters is to be given a great treasure and bulwark against the sorrows of this falling life.

Parents must also be sure to care for their children as a *third priority*. A parent's first priority is to care for one's relationship with God and the second priority is to care for one's spouse in marriage.

Given that the children exist because of the mutual love and embrace of the spouses, that mutual love must be jealously nurtured and guarded against the demands of parenting. Children must be kept in their proper place. One practical example of this is that couples should not abandon their regular dates and times for intimacy because of their children. If we want our children to grow up adoring marriage and desire to pursue it themselves, they must see this modeled to them in the lives of their own parents.

Keeping children in their place also means keeping them out of the marriage bed. Each new child ought to be a welcomed member of the family, but not become the *center* of the family. All of us have visited homes where the children have tragically become the center of the family. The home is strewn with toys in every room. This is a travesty and an injustice done to the children themselves; it nourishes self-centeredness, and deprives the children of learning to share and to respect the boundaries of others.

Husbands and wives also must faithfully parent together, always supporting each other, and seeking common parental goals. Husbands and wives must never disparage each other in front of the children, never allow the other to be disparaged by the children themselves, or use the children as pawns in spousal conflict. Couples ought to be careful to guard against growing emotional distance, and make sure they make time to talk through the challenges of bringing up children. We ought to encourage each other with hope, strengthen each other in patience, and give powerful divine energy to each other via our words. We must never give up, but learn to regularly take a step back from the edge of discouragement and, in the words of St. Sophrony of Essex, "take a cup of tea."

Jewish Midrash, "Childless Love"

There is a beautiful story found in Jewish Midrash entitled "Childless Love." Though children are great blessings from God for the married, not every marriage is blessed with children. What then? The story goes like this:

"A certain Israelite of Sidon, having been married more than ten years without being blessed with children, determined to be divorced from his wife. With this view he brought her before Rabbi Simeon, bar Yochai. The rabbi, who was unfavorably disposed to divorces, tried to dissuade him from it. However, seeing that the man was not inclined to accept his advice, he said this to the couple: 'My children, when you were first joined in the holy bond of wedlock, did you not rejoice? Did you not make a feast and entertain your friends? Now, since ye are resolved to be divorced, let your separation be like your union. Go home, make a feast, entertain your friends, and on the morrow come and I will comply with your wishes.'

"So reasonable a request, coming from such an authority, could not, with any degree of propriety, be rejected. Accordingly, they went home and prepared a sumptuous party to which they invited their friends. During the entertainment the husband, elated with wine, said to his wife: 'My beloved, we have lived together happily these many, many years; it is only the lack of children which makes me want a divorce. To convince you, however, that I bear you no ill-will, I give you permission to take with you out of my house anything you like best.'

"'Be it so,' rejoined the woman.

"As the cup went round the people were merry. Having drunk rather freely, most of the guests fell asleep, among them the master of the feast. The lady no sooner perceived it, then she ordered him to be carried to her father's house, and to be put into a bed she prepared for just that purpose. As the fumes of the wine gradually evaporated, the man awakened.

Finding himself in a strange place, he wondered and exclaimed, 'Where am I? How did I come here? What does this all mean?'

"His wife, who had waited to see the result of her stratagem, stepped from behind a curtain. Begging him not to be alarmed, she told him that he was now in her father's house. 'In your father's house?' Be patient, my dear husband,' replied the prudent woman, 'and I will tell you all. Recollect, did you not tell me last night, I might take out of your house whatever I valued most? Now, believe me, my beloved, among all your treasures there is not one I value so much as I do you; no, there is not a treasure in this world I esteem as much as I do you.'"[5]

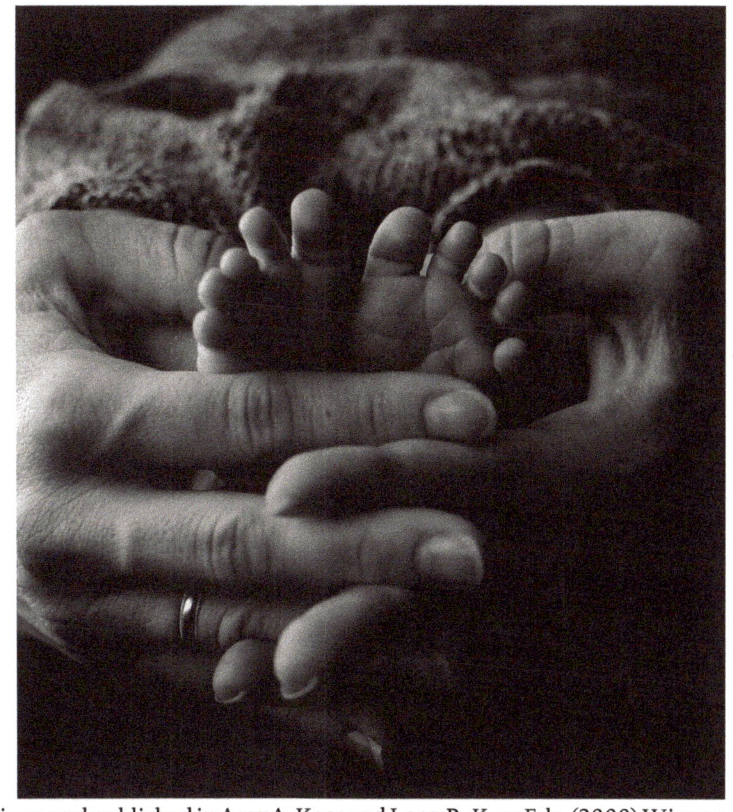

<hr>

5   Taken from Maurice Lamm, The Jewish Way in Love and Marriage, and published in Amy A. Kass and Leon R. Kass Eds. (2000) Wing to Wing, Oar to Oar: Readings on Courting and Marrying, Notre Dame, Indiana: University of Notre Dame Press, pp. 560-561.

Exercises

1 Marriage is a package deal. Why do you think it is difficult for some to accept some parts of the package?

2 Of the three central purposes of marriage, which do you think will be most difficult for you? Which do you think will be the easiest? Why?

- Helpmate/Procreation of Race
- Fruitful Vine
- A Gift from the Lord
- A Quiver Full of Arrows
- Sons and Daughters
- Fruit of the Womb as is Expedient
- Be Fruitful and Multiply
- Offspring like Full Ears of Grain
- Multiply like Jacob and Rachel

Exercises

3 The family dinner table is exceedingly important in family life. How exactly do you plan to use your dinner table?

4 Sometimes parents must give full and undivided attention to their children. When and how do you anticipate doing this?

5 Jesus says that it is better to have a millstone hung around your neck and be cast into the sea than to cause a little one to stumble. How do you think you might cause your own child to stumble if you aren't careful? How can you make sure you don't do this? If you begin to slip and your child knows it, what should you do?

(Continued on the next page)

Scenarios

6 Each night one of your children climbs into your bed in the middle of the night and insists on sleeping with you. This has continued for some months. What do you do?

7 After being married for several years without conceiving, you visit a physician and discover that there is infertility.

How would you react to this news? What are possible positive reasons that God may wish for a couple to face such a challenge?

Scenarios

8 When the first child arrives you discover quickly that your spouse has a much different perspective on parenting than you do. Through discussion it is clear that your parents raised each of you quite differently. Conflicts are multiplying about how to deal with a crying infant, and how to divide the main parenting responsibilities that have arisen. You begin arguing often. What should be done?

9 A couple has two wonderful children, ages 2 and 4. Both pregnancies and deliveries have been complicated and difficult. One day the wife tells her husband that she thinks that two children are enough, and that she isn't sure her body can handle any more children. She would like to stop. The husband has always wanted a large family.

How can this couple work through their disagreement?

ΒΑ
CI
ΛΕΙ
ΟC

7. Roles and Responsibilities

One of the truths that has been obvious to the human race throughout its entire history is that men and women are different and serve different roles in marriage and family life. In all cultures throughout history men and women have had different but complementary relationships to each other, to children, the home, work, hunting, gathering, war, sex, the public, and more. This truth has been obvious to all human cultures in all human ages, except in the present secular and post-Christian Western culture. One of the goals of the secular culture is to burn traditional gender roles to the ground and to enforce an androgynous and unisex perspective upon society. Our culture pursues this even to the point of eviscerating not just tradition, culture and history, but biology itself by affirming that men can have babies and women should become warriors.

The Christian faith teaches that man and woman are fashioned by God as two halves of a whole. Man and woman are incomplete without each other, and their union brings wholeness. Man and woman are equally crowned with glory and honor in the wedding service, but the same divine service also emphasizes uniqueness and complementarity. Both man and woman have unique strengths. Men are physically larger and stronger than women, and are imbued with a disposition to fight, guard, and protect. Women are physically smaller but are uniquely designed by God as givers and nurturers of life. Neurologically, men are assessors, navigators, and strategizers, while women are mind-readers, emotion discerners, and sympathizers. Men are data- and project-focused, while women are person-focused and emotive. The difference between men and women goes down to every single cell in the human body. The full expression of masculinity and femininity in marriage and family life is a means to express the glory of God. Man is encouraged in humility by knowing that he is incomplete without woman, and woman is encouraged in humility by knowing that she was made from and for man.

Gender Roles in the Wedding Epistle

The existence of gender roles in marriage is set forth clearly in the wedding service itself in the Epistle Reading from St. Paul's Letter to the Ephesians. In this reading St. Paul sets forth both common responsibilities of husband and wife, and unique responsibilities of each sex. He writes,

> "Brethren, give thanks always for all things unto God the Father, in the Name of our Lord Jesus Christ; submitting yourselves one to another in the fear of God."

This is what both husband and wife must do in common: give thanks to God constantly and for everything, mutually submit to each other and live in the fear of God.

Having affirmed the roles that are common to husband and wife in marriage, St. Paul details the *unique* gender roles in marriage.

> "Wives, submit yourselves unto your own husbands, as unto the Lord. For the husband is the head of the wife, even as Christ is the head of the Church...as the Church is subject unto Christ, so let the wives be to their own husbands in everything..."

He concludes with,

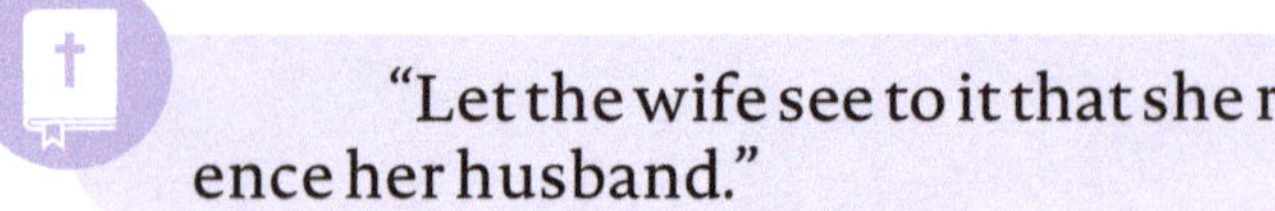

> "Let the wife see to it that she reverence her husband."

While there is a common mutual submission between husbands and wives that expresses itself in serving each other and preferring the other's will above one's own, there is also a unique submission that is the particular role of the wife in marriage. She alone must obey her husband as her head in everything, just as the Church is subject to Christ.

However, in an individualistic culture like ours, obedience is not revered. Many consider obedience to be a form of degradation. This is not God's perspective. The Church teaches that obedience is inescapable. Everyone obeys someone. The difference between enslavement and a life-giving obedience depends on who we obey. Obedience to Jesus is life. Obedience to oneself is death, as is obedience to the passions, sin, and the devil.

While obedience to Jesus is life, it is not easy – especially in the early decades of the Christian life. It is a narrow road that leads to life, a kind of cross-bearing that is life-giving. And so it is for the wife, and so she must learn to respect her husband. Doubtless it will be hard and require great love. And this respect must be given even when the husband is not respectable. Anyone can respect someone when that someone is respectable; there is nothing to praise there. But God is calling wives to respect their husbands even when the husbands are not respectable. This takes the power and presence of the Lord, and it is absolutely central to the fashioning of a Christian marriage and home. This kind of wifely love transforms the lives of husbands. In St. Peter's words this is how a wife can "win" her husband, even if he is disobedient to the word of God. "Wives, be submissive to your own husbands, so that even if any of them are disobedient to the word, they may be won without a word by the behavior of their wives, as they observe your chaste and respectful behavior."[1]

After explaining the unique role of the wife in marriage, St. Paul turns his attention to the duty of the husband and lays out the husband's unique role. He writes,

> "Husbands, love your wives, even as Christ also loved the Church, and gave Himself for her; that he might sanctify and cleanse her with the washing of water by the word, that he might present her to Himself a glorious Church, not having spot, or wrinkle, or any such thing; but that it should be holy and without blemish. So ought men to love their wives as their own bodies. He that loveth his wife loveth himself. For no man ever yet hated his own flesh; but nourisheth and cherisheth it, even as the Lord the Church…let everyone one of you in particular love his wife even as himself."

As much as wives may find it difficult to learn to respect and obey their husbands, they can be very thankful that they are not required to do what every husband is required to do. St. Paul says the husbands must love their wives like Jesus loves the Church. And how is that? First, by dying for her. The husband must give himself for his wife. Second, the husband is called to love his wife by seeking her holiness and purity in everything so that he can present his wife to Christ spotless at the Second Coming. Third, the husband must love his wife as he loves his own flesh. This means he must have as much concern to nourish and cherish his wife as he does his own body. No Christian husband ought to hurt and abuse the body, mind, or heart of his wife any more than he would intentionally hurt his own body, mind, or heart.

Roles and Responsibilities of the Good Husband

The post-Christian culture's embrace of androgyny and unisexism eclipses the beauty of being male

---

and female and in doing so kills marital happiness. The loss of vision for being a husband or a wife has contributed to the progressive decline of marriage and family life as well as a radical increase in cohabitation, out-of-wedlock births, domestic violence, and poverty. With the decline of marriage has come the weakening of the Church on all levels, because the strength of marriage is also the strength of the Church.

The Epistle of the Wedding Service is an excellent place to start thinking about roles and responsibilities in marriage. There are many more beautiful texts in the Sacred Scriptures which elucidate the unique roles of husband and wife. The Good Husband is called by God to be a leader, a domestic pastor, a lover, a provider, and a faithful friend. The Good Wife is called by God to be a helpmate, a homemaker, a lover, a healing drug, the heart of the family, and a faithful friend. These are the basic contours of gender roles in marriage, and husbands and wives ought to encourage each other to nurture and perfect their own callings.[2]

Husbands are called to lead. This is the role of the head, and even if one has a multi-talented wife with many outstanding leadership skills this does not mean that the husband can abandon his calling. Husbands must establish and maintain a vision for marriage. Leadership presupposes vision, and a good husband must develop his vision and pass it on. He must lead in the cultivation of the marriage over time.

The husband is also called to be a lover of his wife, one who takes leadership to ensure that he and his wife haven't just "fallen in love" but "stay in love." The husband is called to nourish and cherish the wife as his love, as his treasure and crown from the Lord. How do we care for treasures and crowns? With great care. As such the husband must never starve his wife of attention, affection, and conversation. He also is called to love his wife unto holiness, always seeking to ennoble her, and to lift her aspirations to the Kingdom of God.

The husband is also called to be the provider for and protector of his family. A mature Christian husband is called to a robust commitment to expend himself in service to his wife and children. In order to do this, he must die to the adolescent

2   For more teaching on the role of The Good Husband and The Good Wife, the reader may listen to the lecture series under the same name at PatristicNectar.org

desire to be perpetually mothered and provided for. He must embrace pain, danger, and responsible risk-taking. This is the unique calling of the man, which is why of the twenty most dangerous professions in the world, nineteen are almost exclusively male. Men must accept shorter life-spans, greater prevalence of disease, and more suffering in order to fulfill their unique roles and responsibilities as husbands. The good husband must assume full responsibility for providing for his family and express this resolve by developing a zealous work-ethic. He must embrace discipline in all areas of his life in order to produce freedom in his family. Wives are not expected by God to equally share responsibility for providing for their families any more than God expects husbands to equally share in pregnancy, labor, birth-pangs, nursing, and all the self-crucifying elements of child-rearing.

Roles and Responsibilities of the Good Wife

The wife is the unique helpmate of her husband. She, like Eve to Adam, is the solution to the "not-good" condition of her husband being alone. No male friend, no job, no hobby, no sport can take the central place of the wife as the one who completes her husband. All of the husband's being longs for his analogue, all of his heart longs for his wife's heart to be with him. The good wife embraces the calling to be her husband's helper, remembering that this is a divine title.

King David says, "God is my helper." In order to be a helper, the wife must accept the leadership of her husband. She must embrace having a head, as the Christian family is not a democracy. This takes courage of heart and is a manifestation of immense feminine power. The good wife will find herself particularly tempted to abandon her position as helper when the husband acts arrogantly, proudly, tyrannically, or somehow threatens or jeopardizes the family through irresponsibility or radical incompetence. Then she will be tempted to fight, raise her voice against her husband, or discourse with him as though she is the head or a co-head. All such actions would disgrace the good wife and set back the effectiveness of her position.

A wife's influence and power lies in her quiet spirit and the inner beauty of her character which especially shows itself in these hours of temptation. A wrong husband, a stupid husband, an incompetent husband, or a foolish husband remains a husband and therefore the head of his wife. It would be easier for any woman to submit to the *perfect or sinless* husband, but that is not what Christian wives are called to do. Humble submission without any fear is how a wife becomes a daughter of Sarah and is the best position from which a wife can help both her husband and her family. The good wife helps her husband by enhancing him, strengthening him, nourishing him, feeding him, adding value to his life and work, energizing him, comforting him, being at his side at all important points, dignifying him, encouraging him, delighting him, cheering him, sobering him, calming him, clothing him, overseeing his health, ensuring his sleep, taming him sexually, being interested in his vocation, counseling him, listening to him, calling him by her own dignity to become a good man and a devoted husband and father. This commitment to being her husband's helper is her primary earthly calling, to which motherhood must be secondary.

The good wife is also the homemaker, that is, the manager of the domestic domain. Work in the home is perhaps the most influential work possible for a family and for the cultivation of Christian culture. St. John Chrysostom says that when the home falters, the city comes to a screeching halt. St. Paul calls upon the older women to teach the younger women not only how to be lovers of their husbands and children, but also workers at home. The Church conceives the home as the most important workplace that exists. It shapes souls and therefore eternity itself, and the good wife is the master of this responsibility. Proverbs 31 shows how varied, complex, multi-faceted, and influential such domestic mastery is. Homemaking is serious business and it involves nutrition, principles of family finance, entrepreneurship, home management theory, child and adolescent development, philosophic and professional issues in home economics, fitting and textiles, interiors and architecture, dynamics of family living, music, painting, gardening, creative recreation, business and finance, and more. The parishes of any land are only as strong as the family homes that make them up.

The good wife is also the heart of the family. As the Most Pure Mother of God is to the Church, so the pious wife is to her own family. As the Theotokos was focused on her heart and taught this to the faithful, so too does the good wife

do this for the family. She encourages her husband and children to bring forth what is good from the good treasure of their hearts. St. Thalassios writes in the *Philokalia* that the woman symbolizes the soul engaged in ascetic practice.[3] The wife dignifies life, builds compassion, reconciles the alienated, and cultivates holiness in the house. She refuses to judge – especially her husband – and teaches others to be non-judgmental as well. In these ways she functions as a spiritual thermostat.

Mutual Agreement on Roles and Responsibilities

While embracing the unique callings from God associated with being a husband or a wife, the couple must also fashion mutual agreement on the discharge of the many practical responsibilities that come with marriage and managing a household. Many of these tasks are not matters of gender roles at all, but matters of competency and willingness, and as such must be negotiated by the couple to their mutual satisfaction. Failing to clarify roles can become a serious cause of disruption and strife. The exercises that follow are designed to facilitate agreements on these roles.

---

3   Vol. 2, Second Century, 27, p. 314, (1981), London: UK, Faber and Faber.

Discussion Questions

Leadership and Respect in the Home

1 How should a wife's respect for her husband manifest itself in practical life? What ways of showing respect for your husband do you think will be easiest for you? What ways will be hardest for you?

2 How can a husband practically manifest "laying down his life" for his wife?

3 What does "headship" mean to you? What are the things that the "head" does in the family that are not done by anyone else?

4 When you hear that the "husband is the head of the wife," are there any *negative ideas or feelings* that arise? If so, what are they? Where do you think they come from?

5 What do you think about day care? When you have children, will you allow them to be watched, supervised, or babysat? If so, by whom and when?

6 What do you think about the wife working outside the home? If so, will the wife work outside the home exactly as the husband does or will it be different?

Discussion Questions

7 What gifts for home life does your spouse have that you yourself do not have?

8 The leadership of a husband does not mean that the husband has more knowledge or talent than his wife. How can a husband lead in those areas that his wife has more skill, talent, or knowledge than himself? How can a wife use her skills and talents in a way that still honors her husband's leadership?

9 What kinds of gender roles did you experience in your family growing up that you admire and wish to emulate?

10 What are the gender roles exhibited in your family of origin that you wish to not imitate?

11 Complete this sentence. "I can best help my mate fulfill his or her role in marriage by...."

12 What are those things that you believe are the primary responsibility of the husband?

13 What are those things that you believe are the primary responsibility of the wife?

Exercises

1 Place these responsibilities on the following continuum (draw a line from the item to the place on the continuum you believe it belongs.)

Wife		Either	Husband
Cooking	Yard work	Taking out trash	Contacting family
Disputes wth neighbors	Doing dishes	Leading prayer	Home repair
RSVP to invitations	Washing cars	Cleaning	Answering the front door

2 A husband has recently come to an important crossroads at work, and has made a decision to accept a new job that will require that the family relocate. He returns home from work and informs his wife that he made the decision and that in two months the family will need to move. The wife is deeply grieved since she was not consulted in the decision, and when she expresses her hurt the husband tells her it is her duty to be submissive. If you were the wife, how could you most constructively respond to this situation? What temptations would present themselves, and how do you think you could overcome them?

Scenarios

3 A wife is finding herself overwhelmed with managing her responsibilities. She is working on an online degree, taking care of the home, and raising two children. She begins to feel that she is drowning and can't keep herself from calling her husband repeatedly at the office asking him to come home and help her with her tasks. The husband asks her to please not call him repeatedly at the office because it is compromising his work and displeasing his employer. The wife feels that he is being insensitive to her predicament. How could the couple move forward to a resolution of this difficulty in a healthy way?

8. Finances

Stewardship in Marriage

Christians believe that they are stewards rather than owners of all that they have, including their very lives. Life itself is a gift from God, as is every breath we take. St. Paul asks,

> "What do you have that you have not received?"[1]

The resources of life as well belong entirely to God, and He entrusts these resources to His people to be used and invested well for His glory and to advance His ennobling causes.

Marriage belongs to God, and He shares it with those Whom He calls to marriage. As St. Paul writes about marriage and monasticism,

> "Everyone has his own calling from God, one in this manner and another in that."[2]

This is why Christian spouses treat their marriages with reverence, and are resolved to care for, deepen and develop their marriages over the course of their lives.

The children born of marriage are also God's. Though He shares the creation of new life with husband and wife, He Himself is the fashioner of children. They belong to Him, and He entrusts them to the couple to be loved and cared for and raised to His glory.

The resources necessary to be married and have a family are also given to us by God as a stewardship. The priest prays specifically for God to provide the resources necessary for the married couple. The priest asks the Lord God in the Betrothal Prayer to,

> "Let Thine Angel go before them all the days of their life."

He chants at the opening of the Crowning Service the words of the

---

1 1 Corinthians 4:7
2 1 Corinthians 7:7

wedding Psalm 127 for the one who fears the Lord,

> "Thou shalt eat of the fruit of thy labors: O blessed art thou, and happy shalt thou be."

In the first Crowning Prayer, the priest asks God to,

> "Give them of the dew of heaven from on high, and of the fatness of the earth. Fill their houses with wheat, wine and oil and with every good thing, so that they may give in turn to those in need."

The priest prays for home resources for the newlyweds so that, like the Church itself, their home might be a center of almsgiving. In the second Crowning Prayer, the priest again prays that God would give the couple "sufficiency in all things" so that they may "abound in every good work." In the Prayer for the Removing of the Crowns, the priest prays that the Lord might "replenish their lives with good things." Finally, the Nuptial Blessing that concludes the wedding service blesses the newly-married couple to receive, among other beautiful things, "prosperity of life" and an "abundance of earthly good things."

God provides for those He has called to marriage all the resources they need in His providential will to accomplish the sacred tasks He has arranged for them. This is a reality that should give to the couple great confidence and peace. They are not in marriage alone, but with God Himself.

The Presence of Jesus Expressed in Family Finances

One of the areas that marriages can demonstrate that they are truly Christian is in the area of money. Luxury is not Christian. Jesus teaches us that our riches should be in heaven where our hearts are to be focused. We are sojourners on this earth. No earthly possessions last. God gives resources and money to His people not only to provide for their legitimate needs, but to enable them to serve others and help the poor. As such, the Church Fathers teach that riches are given to couples in order to be shared. When we are greedy and demand luxuries, we are actually stealing from the needy whom God intends us to bless on His behalf. Possessions and real estate are justified by their use in service to God and others. St. John Chrysostom teaches, for instance, that the family home should be the size the family actually needs. He says it should fit like a comfortable shoe – being neither too small so that the smallest movements cause pain nor too large so that we trip and fall.[3] It is natural for Christian spouses to downsize when their children are grown and the true financial needs of the family decrease. The prized Christian standard is dispossession – something that death will involuntarily accomplish for all of us, but can be a virtue when voluntarily embraced for the sake of following Christ as seen in the dispossession of our monks and nuns.

Pious married couples can also show great virtue with regards to money and finances by practicing generosity and contentment. I once met an elderly Christian man who shared a story with me about the financial principles that he and his wife established when they were first married. They made a mutual agreement to tithe 10% of their gross income to God from the start no matter what limited standard of living the remaining 90% would allow them. They also discussed in detail what kind of standard of living they would be content not to go above in the future should God so bless them that they could reach this pinnacle. They made these agreements in detail about the kind of house, car, etc. that they would be content with. The man was very pleased to tell me that though it was quite difficult for him and his wife to strictly tithe 10% from the start they did it nonetheless, living on 90% of their gross income. Over time, God blessed their hard work and virtuous adherence to Scripture's financial principles, and the couple was able to live on 10% of their income and give away 90% of their resources to church and charity. This is the kind of impact for the Kingdom of God that is possible when a couple's finances are placed beneath the feet of Jesus.

Conflict over Finances in Marriage

Despite this fundamental reality, it is also true that the issue of resources, particularly conflict over financial management, is today one of the prime reasons cited by divorcing couples for their abandonment of marriage. There are many reasons that the use of money can cause marital conflict. Couples often bring to their union different attitudes concerning money that they have previously learned from their respective family cultures, years of being on their own, career scenes, and more. Besides these different perspectives of money and its use, there are also often differences in virtue with regards to money.

Money and its use is a topic that Jesus often addresses. The use of money is a spiritual matter, and couples often may be at different places in their spiritual development with regards to the stewardship of financial resources. Avarice, the love of money, is a root of all kinds of evil.[4] Its potential for the utter destruction of marriage should not be underestimated. For this reason couples preparing for marriage are wise to thoroughly discuss the subject of finances in order to renew their Christian commitment to being faithful stewards of the financial resources that the Lord provides them, and to form a common mind on how they will manage their money.

Financial Oneness

One of the most important Biblical principles that a couple needs to embrace in marriage is the principle of financial oneness. Christian marriage takes two people and makes them one flesh. For a married couple there is simply no "mine" and "yours" in any area at all. St. Paul reveals this truth strikingly by affirming that the very *bodies* of the couple belong to the other.

> "The wife does not have authority over her own body, but the husband does; and likewise the husband does not have authority over his own body, but the wife does."[5]

The oneness of marriage is likewise expressed in the sharing of the common cup in the wedding service. In receiving the cup from the hands of the priest the couple pledges to receive all that comes in their common life – both plenty and want – *together*. It is an unhealthy practice for couples to maintain two financial systems in their home, to have "my account" and "your account." There is no financial "mine" and "yours" in Christian marriage. All assets are shared in common, and all debts are mutual. For this reason, the Church does not permit couples to sign "prenuptial" financial agreements. These agreements in principle deny the oneness that marriage creates, and are a set-up for divorce. Financial oneness also means that the couple agrees to use their resources only by mutual agreement. Mutual agreement requires compromise, and then obedience to hold to the agreement even if one of the parties is tempted to violate it. An agreement is only as effective as it is kept. This is the place to start when trying to establish your family's financial practices: everything by mutual agreement.

It should also be pointed out here that the traditional role of husband as primary breadwinner does not mean that the money he is paid belongs to him any more than it belongs to the wife.

Conversely, the wife who manages the home and raises the children does not own the home or children any more than the husband does. Good husbands know that they cannot work successfully *outside the home* without their wives taking care of the most important work of all *in the home*. And good wives and mothers know that the zealous work ethic of their husbands outside the home is completely focused on providing for them and the children. The two efforts are complementary – this is how we support each other.

The Scriptures also reveal the many businesses and financial arrangements in which a wife and mother may be involved from within the home itself. Home business has become a massive form of commerce today, and can often provide resources and educational opportunities for wives and children in the context of the family home.

Establishing Financial Principles of Your Family

It is important now – while you are preparing for marriage – to flesh-out the following financial principles:

· Tithing[6]. The Scriptures teach that the first fruits belong to God. We return back to God the first portion of what He gives to us as an expression of thanksgiving and an acknowledgement that we have received everything from Him. The first "bill" to be paid each month should be your stewardship pledge to your local parish.

· Debt.[7] The Scriptures teach that debt is a dangerous form of slavery. Credit card debt, amassed often as an outworking of consumerist passion and a failure to deny oneself what one cannot afford, is a common source of conflict in marriage. While some form of debt may be judged wise in order to obtain an appreciating asset like a home, most debt should be avoided. All debt should be assumed only by mutual agreement of the spouses.

· Living Within Your Means. The Scriptures teach the principle of contentment. Believers are to be content with what God provides them, and contain their appetites accordingly. No amount of income creates happiness, and no lack of income can steal joy for believers. Our treasure is elsewhere, in heaven. If we cannot learn to be happy and content while living within our means, we will not ever be happy. Nothing is ever *enough* for the greedy.

· Budgeting. Budgeting is the mature way to keep financial stress at its lowest. Documenting exact income and expenses allows the couple to have perspective, to discern the lay of the financial land. Holding to a budget will enable a couple from falling into financial trouble, as well as ensuring a stability of life that is precious. Budgeting is responsibility in action, and it enables couples to make sure they are using their financial resources according to their vision. Without a budget money tends to "disappear."

---

6   For more on tithing read the Prophecy of Malachi
7   For more on debt read the Proverbs of Solomon

• Saving. The Scriptures promote savings. St. Paul says,

"Children are not responsible to save up for their parents, but parents for their children."[8]

Denying the insatiable appetite for acquisition in order to save money is the way that couples can be enabled to give substantial gifts to the Church, to the needy, and to their own children. Saving money is not something for rich people. Saving money is a virtue that should be employed regardless of one's income. It is accomplished by self-denial. The placement of savings in this or that investment is something that should be mutually agreed upon.

• Use of Disposable Income. Disposable income is the income that a couple uses each month *after* they have paid their needs. Needs are tithes to God, bills for reasonable food, housing, savings, etc. If a couple has money left over after paying these essentials, they have money for their wants. Distinguishing needs from wants is basic to mature financial management. Couples should agree together on the use of whatever disposable income they have.

• Gift-Giving. Christians believe that it is "more blessed to give than to receive." For this reason gift-giving is at the very heart of the Christian home. Supporting extended family, neighbors, fellow church members, clergy and monastics, local charities, and more is simply our way of life. Couples are wise to discuss their mutual gift-giving both for their own family in Christmas and birthday gift-giving, and for others so that all is done wisely and no good endeavor is stained by discord.

• Management of Accounts. The day-to-day management of accounts, credit cards, and payments can grow to significant size as a family grows. Each spouse brings a different skill set to the family, and it is important for the spouses to agree together on who will manage the books, and what that entails. If one spouse is skilled financially or another particularly inept, then the task assignments are easy to make. However, it is important for the one who assumes responsibility for financial management to keep the other informed and up to date. This may take some education and explanation, but taking the time to do this is wise and nurtures mutuality.

The Learning Curve of Financial Responsibility

If a couple marries young, then the learning curve for establishing and maintaining a household can be extreme. Moving from your parents' home into your own often means discovering a host of bills and financial responsibilities you did not know existed. Insurances, taxes, utilities, upkeep and maintenance, food costs, and more will abound quickly. Even if the newlyweds lived on their own for a while before marrying, there will be many new realities and adjustments that must be made.

No one is born a financial expert, and everyone makes mistakes sometimes. Financial mistakes in marriage are often made by one person but the pain is inflicted upon both, and even on the whole family if the couple has children. It is important to be honest and admit when you have made a mistake. Don't try to cover it up. A large dose of graciousness and abundant forgiveness is often called for in the early years of marriage and it will encourage honesty. Prepare yourself ahead of time to bestow it. Remember the law of Christ our Master:

> "Do unto others as you would like them to do unto you."[9]

If you are gracious when your spouse makes a financial mistake, you are paving the ground for your spouse to be gracious to you when you make a similar or worse mistake.

Exercises

1 *Reviewing Personal Histories Concerning Financial Principles*
Every husband and wife brings to the marriage a personal history from his or her family of origin concerning the acquisition and use of financial resources. Talk together about what principles were practiced in each other's families concerning:

Tithing to God and the Church | Debt | Savings | Budgeting
Maintaining Accounts | Gift-Giving | The Use of Credit Cards

What are the positives from each person's family history in these areas? What are the negatives?

Exercises

Creating Your Budget

2 Sit down together and write out your first draft budget. Find out what expenses are common to the other, but totally unknown by you. After you have fleshed out a bare bones budget, place the bills in order of importance. Then write down the total sum of your combined income, and assess if your income currently meets your projected needs.

Take the time to come to an agreed upon figure for each of the major areas: tithing, housing, food, utilities, etc.

Take note of the areas where you must do more research, as well as the areas that are basic to your partner but not basic to you, and vice versa. Decide how you will address these areas of difference.

Lastly, discuss how you will respond to a violation of the budget by either of you or both. How will you rectify the budget if it has been damaged?

Exercises

3

Debt

A common mistake that couples make is that, as their financial income and resources increase over time, their "needs" increase. Often couples will leverage themselves to the maximum in order to maintain the highest standard of living, and this approach to finances becomes normative resulting in the "curse of the golden handcuffs." Even wealthy people can be oppressed by personal debt and by refusing to settle on a standard of living and practice contentment, and so they amass debt and feel like slaves even though the chains are made of gold. Discuss together what standard of living you both would be content with.

What kind of house?

What kind of cars?

What kind of disposable income?

Can you make an agreement that when you reach that standard of living you will agree not to increase it over time, but rather divert this increased income in the future to the needs of others? If you cannot make that agreement, why do you think you are unable to?

Scenarios

4 While the husband is at work and the wife at home, she is visited by a salesman at the door. He is offering her a subscription to a number of magazines and discount journals that are "guaranteed to save the family up to 25% on their monthly bills." She is hesitant because the subscription is $199, but the salesman says this is a major discount from normal costs and the sale ends that day. She finally ignores her hesitance, and makes the purchase. When the husband comes home, she informs him of her purchase, and he is distressed. She has broken their agreement not to spend over $50 without mutual agreement, and the family does not have $199 free to cover this cost. The plot thickens when the following day fraudulent charges appear on the credit card that she used to make the purchase. The husband is close to blowing his top. The wife is ashamed. What should each of them do?

Scenarios

5 A couple that has been married peacefully for five years falls into a difficult spot when the husband loses his job. He has unemployment income, but it is not enough to sustain the family. He insists on making significant cuts to many areas of their budget, which the wife begrudgingly accommodates. Soon, however, the anxiety of the husband increases to the extent that he asks for his wife's debit and credit cards, and tells her she is not allowed to make any purchases whatsoever without his explicit permission. What counsel would you give to the husband? What counsel would you give to the wife?

6 After ten years of marriage, the sister and brother-in-law of the wife experience a terrible health crisis that leaves them on the verge of losing their family home. The wife wants to help her sister and brother and law by taking $20,000 that the couple has saved for the college education of their children and giving it to her sister. The husband does not think this is fair to their children, and opposes this gift. He doesn't want his sister and brother-in-law to suffer, but cannot agree to help them in the way his wife is asking. They are at loggerheads. How might they climb out of this predicament?

9. Spiritual Life

The Spiritual Potential of Christian Marriage

Jesus Christ calls upon all of His disciples to,

> "Seek first the Kingdom of God and His righteousness."[1]

This is the top priority for all Christians. For believers, the Kingdom is supreme. The presence of the Kingdom of God on the earth radically changes everything about our lives, including marriage. Christian marriage is no longer primarily focused on the things of the earth but upon the heavenly kingdom. Married Christians do not pine after earthly blessings but heavenly ones. Heaven has invaded all the trappings of earthly marriage and turned the focus upwards such that married Christians bring the magnetism of the Kingdom to every part of their lives: their relationship, sex life, home, real estate, possessions, children, work, and more.

St. John Chrysostom explains that New Covenant man has been ennobled and received more divine aid than Old Covenant man, and at the same time the ethical bar has been greatly elevated. This is how we are to understand Jesus' command that His followers must surpass the righteousness of the scribes and the Pharisees. Christ has transformed human capacity without changing fundamental human nature. It is like iron coming into contact with fire: the iron becomes fire, but retains its own nature. With the coming of the Holy Spirit at Pentecost, St. Chrysostom affirms that the flesh of man has become lighter,

> "wholly spiritual...crucified in all parts,"

and

> "flying with the same wings as the soul."[2]

---

1   St. Matthew 6:33
2   St. John Chrysostom, Homily 13 on Romans, NPNF, Vol. 11, p. 435.

This transformation is what has rendered self-denial possible. The Old Covenant ways of living, including the areas of marriage and sexuality, are now beneath New Covenant man. St. John Chrysostom says,

"Since we have been vouchsafed a larger and more perfect teaching, God having no longer spoken by the prophets, but 'having in these last days spoken to us by His Son,' let us show forth a conversation far higher than theirs, and suitable to the honor bestowed on us. Strange would it be that He should have so far lowered Himself, as to choose to speak to us no longer by His servants, but by His own mouth, and yet we should show forth nothing more than those of old. They had Moses for their teacher, we, Moses' Lord. Let us then exhibit a heavenly wisdom worthy of this honor and let us have nothing to do with the earth."[3]

This heavenly orientation – to have nothing to do with the earth – is uniquely Christian, and must manifest itself in all aspects of married life.

In the New Covenant, marriage, like monasticism, has immense spiritual potential. Christian marriage is a pathway of salvation, a cauldron of transformation, a mystery of love, an ascetic road of repentance, and an arena for spiritual contest. The late-antique ecclesiastical writer Tertullian, in his *Letter to His Wife*, elaborates on the depth of spiritual union possible in a truly Christian marriage. In a tender and poetic portrayal of marriage, he lauds the type of Christian marriage over which Jesus Christ rejoices. He writes,

"Where the flesh is one, one is the spirit too. Together they pray, together prostrate themselves, together perform their fasts; mutually teaching, mutually exhorting, mutually sustaining. Equally are they both found in the Church of God; equally at the banquet of God; equally in straits; in persecutions, in refreshments. Neither hides from the other; neither shuns the other; neither is troublesome to the other; the sick is visited, the indigent relieved, with freedom. Alms are given without danger of torment; sacrifices without scruple; daily diligence without impediment; there is no stealthy singing, no trembling greeting, no mute benediction. Between the two echo psalms and hymns; and they mutually challenge each other which shall better chant to their Lord. Such things when Christ sees and hears, He joys. To these He sends His own peace. Where two are, there withal is He Himself. Where He is, there the evil one is not."

Here is an authentic vision of Christian marriage. It is no mere earthly union serving worldly ends nor fixated upon physical rewards. Christian marriage is a spiritual ascesis, a life-context for worship, prayer, fasting, almsgiving, visitation, hospitality, and suffering, a training ground of the soul just as monasticism is, and leading to salvation. Among other things, marriage is designed by God to perfect the character of its participants. Clement of Alexandria describes the spiritual opportunities for the development of virtue provided by marriage. He writes,

"The particular characteristic of the married state is that it gives the man who desires a perfect marriage an opportunity to take responsibility for everything in the home which he shares with his wife. The apostle says that one should appoint bishops who by their oversight of their own house have learned to be in charge of the whole church...The prize in the contest of men is won by him who has trained himself by the discharge of the duties of husband and father and by the supervision of a household, regardless of pleasure and pain – by him, I say, who in the midst of his solicitude for his family shows himself inseparable from the love of God and rises superior to every temptation which assails him through children and wife and...possessions."

Describing the Saints in Paradise, St. John Chrysostom writes,

"There are choirs of virgins, there are assemblies of widows, there are fraternities of those who shine in holy wedlock; in short, many are the degrees of virtue."[4]

Christian marriage is a salvific ideal. It is possible for a married couple to attain great virtue, even to rival monastics. In a duly famous homily in which he gave vast counsels for Christian marriage, St. John Chrysostom writes,

"If any marry thus, with these views, he will be but little inferior to monks; the married but a little below the unmarried."[5]

How sad is it that this ideal is so rarely achieved in today's world! So many Christians lack a true vision for the spiritual potential of Christian marriage. We have not been catechized and formed with a Christian vision for marriage, but rather we have been unwittingly malformed by the pervasive vision for relationships and sexuality that is so popular in secular culture.

---

4   Homily 30 on 1 Corinthians, NPNF, Vol. 12, pp. 178-179

5   Homily 20 on Ephesians, NPNF, Vol. 13, p. 151

Marital interaction is the arena of spiritual acquisition and progress. St. Tikhon of Zadonsk speaks to this when he writes,

> "The husband and wife must lay virtue, and not passion, as the foundation of their love, that is, when the husband sees any fault in his wife, he must nudge her meekly, and the wife must submit to her husband in this. Likewise when a wife sees some fault in her husband, she must exhort him, and he is obliged to hear her."[6]

Quotes from the Rite of Crowning on the Spiritual Life of the Couple

One of the central petitions in the litanies that adorn both the beginning of the Betrothal Service and the beginning of the Crowning Service is a petition asking God to preserve the couple

> "in oneness of mind and in steadfastness of faith."

This is followed by a petition that God give them a "blameless life" and yet another for an "honorable marriage." Much of the service is absorbed in praying that the married couple would progress in virtue in and through their marriage.

In the first main prayer of the betrothal service, we also pray that God would guide the couple "unto every good work." Good works are what each Christian is fashioned for. As St. Paul says,

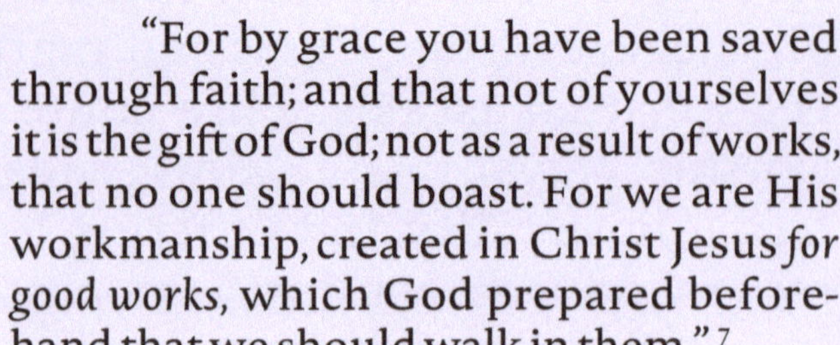

> "For by grace you have been saved through faith; and that not of yourselves it is the gift of God; not as a result of works, that no one should boast. For we are His workmanship, created in Christ Jesus *for good works*, which God prepared beforehand that we should walk in them."[7]

Every Christian is saved in order to do good works, and every marriage is fashioned by God and established in order to be a factory of good deeds. This is why we pray for the couple to be guided "unto every good work."

In the Great Prayer of Betrothal, the celebrants and congregation ask that God establish the married couple in four distinct things: faith, oneness of mind, truth, and love. The priest prays that God's angel would go before them all the days of their life. The married are to trod the way of love, truth and faith and follow the angels.

---

6   (1991, 1994) translated by Fr. George Lardas, Journey to Heaven, Jordanville: Holy Trinity Monastery, p. 117.

7   Ephesians 2:8-10

Practical Guidance for Spiritual Life in Marriage

#1. Maintain Your Relationships in Proper Priority.

Jesus is to be our "first love."[8] His presence as King and Lord in the individual life of both husband and wife is what is necessary for any marriage to be Christian. We should never compromise our relationship to Christ and the Church for the sake of another human being or relationship. Jesus does not accept second place in anyone's life. If Jesus is second or third this simply means there are idols in our lives that must be destroyed. After the Lord comes our first 'earthly love': our spouse. Following the priority of our spouse comes our children. Following our children comes the priority of work and other relationships. This is the order that must be preserved in order for spiritual life to prosper:

1. Jesus
2. Your Spouse
3. Your Children
4. Work and Other Relationships

#2 Live a Church-Centered Life Together.

The chief way that married couples express the supreme priority of Jesus in their lives is by enshrining worship and *koinonia* (fellowship) in their marriage. All good things flow from the altar. Believers can imagine their lives as having a large elastic band around their waists that encircles them and the holy table. They draw near to commune with God, and then as they leave to go to work, or school, or home they are always drawn back to the altar and to the house of God. Christian couples ought commit themselves to faithful attendance at worship on Sundays and all Great Feasts, and agree together how they will serve their local parish and use their gifts in ministry.

#3 Family Prayer.

While husband and wife should always maintain their own personal prayer discipline, it is exceedingly important for husbands, wives, and children to pray together in fixed family prayer. Each couple must order their family prayer by establishing a *domestic typikon*. The Church has a *typikon* that arranges all the details of corporate prayer. This is a model that can be imitated by husbands and wives in principle by agreeing to pray together at certain fixed times, like before and after meals, in the evening before bed, as well as asking each other's forgiveness at the conclusion of evening prayer, blessing each other with the sign of the cross in bed before falling asleep, arranging for and preparing confession with their spiritual father at least once a month, keeping the fast and giving the alms made available by fasting, reading together the Scriptures and appropriate Patristic literature, maintaining a dignified prayer corner, inviting the priest to bless the home each year after Theophany, and practicing hospitality. The Scriptures say that "two are better than one" and this certainly proves itself in the

---

8   Revelation 2:6

mutual encouragement that husband and wife can provide each other in the spiritual life. When pursuing a common quest for the Kingdom of God, it is possible for Christian couples to turn their homes into small domestic churches.

#4 *Choose a Mutual Spiritual Father and Keep Close to Him.*

Having a spiritual father is a tremendous blessing from the Lord Himself, as He is the One who gives us pastors to shepherd our souls. It is not always possible for the couple to have the same spiritual father, but this is a special blessing if it can be accomplished. Staying in regular contact with the spiritual father for confession and guidance is a key to long-term marital happiness, and provides an immense sense of support and encouragement in family life.

#5 *Respect Each Other's Conscience.*

Even in the most united marriages where two hearts beat virtually as one, both husband and wife maintain his or her individual conscience. It is common for there to be differences of opinion on spiritual matters, and respecting the conscience of the other is a basic expression of love and freedom. A spouse should never ask the other to compromise his or her conscience before God for any reason, even if one spouse considers the conviction of the other spouse to be immature or an expression of weakness. We are called to bear each other's burdens in a milieu of mutual respect.

What to Do if You Are Unequally Yoked

While Christians are only permitted to marry Christians, it sometimes happens that for various reasons a husband or wife will find themselves in a marriage that is, in the words of St. Paul, "unequally yoked." This language means that sometimes Christian husbands and wives may find themselves married to a partner who either has never been a Christian, has ceased to remain a Christian, or is a very weak Christian. Believers should never practice "missionary dating" by dating someone who is not a believer with the hopes that through the relationship the unbeliever or the uncommitted Christian will become a dedicated follower of Jesus. St. Paul writes to the Church in Corinth about situations where only one spouse in the marriage had become Christian. These unequally yoked believers asked the Apostle if they should leave the marriage. His response was this,

> "If any brother has a wife who is an unbeliever, and she consents to live with him, let him not send her away. And a woman who has an unbelieving husband, and he consents to live with her, let her not send her husband away...For how do you know, O wife, whether you will save your husband? Or how do you know, O husband, whether you will save your wife?"[9]

Living faithfully in an unequally yoked condition is often a significant Cross, but the presence of the Kingdom of God here and now with and in us enables us to follow Christ and to bear the Cross unto salvation. We can love our faithless spouses and do constant secret good in their name before the face of God.

What to Do if You Are Living Together before Marriage

It is very common in our secular culture for couples to live together before marriage, even in place of marriage altogether. If you are currently living together while preparing for marriage, it is extremely important to make a significant change. Living together outside of marriage is considered a serious sin by the Church. It is fornication, and is a practical assault on marriage itself. When a couple lives together outside of marriage, they are plundering the goods of marriage, since these goods have not yet been granted to them by God. Besides the damage that the sin of living together does to the spiritual lives of the couple and the offense it makes to the Lord God, it is also a major contributor to eventual divorce. The statistics on the success of marriages preceded by the couple living together are grim. What to do? The first thing to do is to repent, and to both go to confession and accept the penance that the father confessor gives. The second thing to do is to separate and remain separate – no matter how difficult the task – until you are married in the Church. By respecting the Lord's commandment, the Church's guidance, and each other in this way you will be greatly blessed and begin your marriage on the right footing.[10]

---

9   1 Cor. 7:12-13, 16

10   If the cohabiting couple has children together the spiritual father may direct them to procure civil marriage while they prepare themselves spiritually to be crowned in the Church.

Exercises

1   *Discerning the Uniqueness of Christian Marriage*

Since the presence of the Kingdom of God has greatly elevated the lives of God's people, how is being a Christian going to impact your marriage with regards to:

	With Faith in Christ	Without Faith
Real Estate		
Possessions		
Sickness		
Sex		
Children		
Career		
Extended Family		

How would your approach to these subjects be different if Jesus had not conquered death, defeated the devil, atoned for sin, and given you the Holy Spirit?

Exercises

2   ### Mutually Supporting Each Other's Spiritual Life

Tertullian, in his Letter to His Wife, presents an inspiring vision of "spiritual togetherness." He uses the words "together," "mutually," and "equally" each 3 times in his affirmation that where the flesh is one, "one is the spirit too."

On a scale of 1 to 10, where would you rate your "togetherness" in spiritual things at this moment?

Where are you strong in your mutual spiritual life?

Where do you need improvement?

3   ### Exhorting and Correcting Each Other

St. Tikhon of Zadonsk writes that when the husband sees any fault in his wife he ought "nudge her meekly" and the wife, if she sees some fault in her husband, must "exhort him, and he is obliged to hear her." This mutual exhortation is rooted and enabled, he writes, by laying a foundation of their love in "virtue" and not "passion."

Does gentle correction already exist in your relationship? If yes, cite a few examples.

If no, how can gentle and sensitive interaction become normal for you?

How would you best hear a "nudge" or an "exhortation"?

Exercises

4 Establishing the Typikon and Prayer Discipline in Your Domestic Church

In order to nourish a significant spiritual life in your family, you must formally establish its contours. Write out your own Typikon with the help of the questions below:

When will you pray together?

When you pray, what exactly will you pray?

Where will you do this prayer?

When will you go to church?

When you go, how will you be on time?

What ministry or service do you wish to fulfill in your local parish?

How often will you confess? Who will make the arrangements with your confessor?

When will you entertain guests in your home? How will you decide on this? Will you invite the needy and not just your friends?

Where do you need improvement?

Scenarios

5 After some years of marriage during which prayer and church were central, your spouse loses interest in attending church. He/she begins to spend less time at home, and more time with friends he/she had before marriage. He/she is no longer interested in nourishing the spiritual lives of the children, and has come to think that fasting is meaningless and too much work.
What are some constructive responses that you might pursue in light of this?

How can you help your spouse rekindle his/her first love?

What are some damaging responses that, if in this situation, you would like to avoid?

10. Enduring to the End

Christian Marriage is Forever

It is one thing to *get* married. It is another to *stay* married. Christian marriage is forever. It is an expression of a love that never fails. It is fashioned after the image of the mystical marriage between God and His People, between Christ and the Church which knows no end but only a continual deepening and mutual interpenetration. Though the common contours of earthly marriage such as pairing off and separation from others, sexual intercourse, a common house, and the bearing and raising children all cease with the passing of earthly life, the core of Christian marriage, what St. John Chrysostom calls a "union of souls", is designed by God to remain forever. In *this sense*, Christian marriage is eternal.

The "foreverness" of marriage is expressed liturgically by the use of rings and removal of crowns by the priest at the conclusion of the wedding service. The exchange of rings is an ancient and cherished portion of the betrothal service. The prayers in the betrothal service mention rings as an expression of power (Patriarch Joseph), glory (Prophet Daniel), the revelation of moral uprightness (Righteous Tamar), bountiful love (Prodigal Son), and God's heavenly benediction. The rings – in their circular design – are also symbolic of eternality, and are to manifest the indissoluble love of the couple married together in the Lord. At the conclusion of the wedding service, just before the bestowal of the final and great Nuptial Blessing, the priest removes the crowns of the newly-married couple with these words,

"Receive their crowns into thy kingdom, preserving them spotless, blameless, and without reproach unto ages of ages. Amen."

The priest asks God to receive and preserve forever the crowns of the couple. There is a beautiful custom in some Orthodox traditions that the husband is buried with the crown of his wife in his hand, and the wife is buried with the crown of the husband in her hand, expressing that they go to the Kingdom as married believers (just as monastics go as monastics), and so that following the Resurrection they can place them on each other's head in the Kingdom of God.

Staying Married

The Christian ideal of one marriage for life and eternity has long been a well-known and respected reality for most of Christian history. That is no longer the case. We who live in the post-Christian West live another reality today. We live in a culture that has less respect for the solemn obligations of marriage than for the simplest business contract. The Sexual Revolution brought with it the degradation of marriage not only in the legalization of adultery and the promotion of premarital sex, but in the embrace of so-called "no-fault divorce." In such a milieu, monogamy has lost its meaning and now does not mean one partner for life, but means having one sexual partner (to whom you may or may not be married) at a time. Many Americans have been married and divorced multiple times, but consider themselves monogamous for being married to only one person at a time.

One of the great shocks to Greek and Jewish culture that the Lord Jesus Christ brought in His teaching was His strict forbiddance of divorce.

"Whoever divorces his wife and marries another woman commits adultery against her; and if she herself divorces her husband and marries another man, she is committing adultery." [1]

Christians are not to divorce. In fact, the Prophet Malachi reveals the Lord's Word on divorce this way,

"I hate divorce, says the Lord, the God of Israel." [2]

There is a small exception to the absolute forbiddance of divorce in the Church for the cause of serious sins like adultery and apostasy. But this small exception can never become the rule in the Church, and it does not come with any guarantee of permission for contracting another marriage. That is a separate matter altogether, and when it is granted by the bishop, the Church has a special service for the second marriage of divorcees during which the couple does not

---

1   St. Mark 10:11-12
2   Malachi 2:16

receive the standard crowning prayers of glory, but rather the priest petitions the Lord God for forgiveness for the couple who was unable to endure sexual temptation and for whom it has become "better to marry than to burn."[3] The goal in staying married is not to untie what God has tied. In Jesus' words,

"What God has joined together, let no man separate."[4]

How is it to be done? How can two sinners who live together persevere in marriage to the end? The answer to this question is the same as the answer to the question for every believer: how will I persevere in my faith to the end? Jesus constantly calls upon His disciples to persevere to the end.

"The one who endures to the end will be saved."[5]

Staying married to the end is just as possible as remaining a faithful Christian to the end and being saved. It is only accomplished by the grace of God, and by the collaboration with God by the faithful in repentance and faith. St. Paul writes,

"I thank my God always concerning you, for the grace of God which was given you in Christ Jesus, that in everything you were enriched in Him, in all speech and all knowledge...so that you are not lacking in any gift, awaiting eagerly the revelation of our Lord Jesus Christ, who shall also confirm you to the end, blameless in the day of our Lord Jesus Christ. God is faithful, through whom you were called into fellowship with His Son, Jesus Christ our Lord."[6]

Our confidence is in the faithfulness of God. Our hope is in the help of our Lord Jesus Who will confirm both our faith and our marriages to the end.

Exercising great concern to maintain our faith and our marriages is the path to preserving and developing both. There is no passage of Holy Scripture that more poignantly warns against the perils of losing one's faith and salvation than St. Paul's Epistle to the Hebrews. These Hebrew Christians were on the verge of abandoning their Christian faith and returning to Judaism. St. Paul issues numerous warnings to these believers against betraying Jesus and apostatizing.

---

3   1 Corinthians 7
4   St. Mark 10:9
5   St. Matthew 10:22, 24:13
6   1 Corinthians 1:4-6, 8-9

No less than six different times in the 13 chapters of this epistle does St. Paul issue his stern warnings:

• "For this reason we must pay much closer attention to what we have heard, lest we drift away from it" (2:1-4)

• "Take care, brethren, lest there should be in any one of you an evil, unbelieving heart, in falling way from the living God, but encourage one another day after day" (3:7-19)

• "Let us be diligent to enter that rest, lest anyone fall through…disobedience" (4:11-16)

• "Let us press on to maturity" (6:1)

• "Let us hold fast the confession of our hope without wavering, for He who promised is faithful; and let us consider how to stimulate one another to love and good deeds…encouraging one another all the more as you see the day drawing near" (10:19-39)

• "Strengthen the hands that are weak and the knees that are feeble, and make straight paths for your feet, so that the limb which is lame may…be healed…See to it that no one comes short of the grace of God; that no root of bitterness springing up causes trouble…that there be no immoral or godless person like Esau who sold his own birthright for a single meal… See to it that you do not refuse Him Who is speaking…let us show gratitude, by which we may offer to God an acceptable service with reverence and awe, for our God is a consuming fire" (12:12-29).

In these six apostolic warnings against giving up one's faith, we find the recipe not only for remaining Christians but for persevering in our marriages: pay close attention to the development of your marriage, take care of it like the precious gift it is, watch over your heart lest it change for the worse, be diligent in developing your union, don't let it stagnate but press on to maturity in your relationship, encourage each other day by day, stimulate each other to love and good deeds more and more as the end draws nearer each day, strengthen the weak portions, heal the diseased aspects, don't allow bitterness to grow, don't be a godless pleasure-lover and abandon your marriage for a single fling, listen to God's voice, show Him your gratitude for what He has given you, and remember that you are called to serve Him above all with reverence and awe.

This is how you keep divorce far away from you. In a culture awash in divorce, the Christian couple needs a firm resolve and intentionality to persevere together to the end. Divorce is almost never a profitable corrective. The proverbial grass often seems greener on the other side, but it rarely is. Christians know that dry times come and dry times go, and that fairy-tale marriages are phony. Believers learn over time how to endure affliction, often through the great teachers which are aging and sickness. We learn that we can thrive and grow and love even with pain and some measure of suffering. In fact, we learn that cross-bearing is life-giving. If we keep our eyes on the prize of our high calling then we can endure, with God's help, all things. We can do all things through Christ Who strengthens us.

Is It Possible to Recover After Infidelity?

Infidelity is perhaps the greatest form of betrayal in marriage, and for many couples it is the end altogether. Though infidelity destroys many a marriage, there are many couples who have not only survived infidelity but have come through the painful process of repentance and rebuilding trust after betrayal into a new and deeper marriage commitment. This rebuilding and rebirth can only take place conscientiously and with important guidance and counsel. Learning to establish boundaries, appreciating when men and women cannot simply be "friends", and watching out for the growth of improper intimacy at work, in your neighborhood, on the internet or with ex-partners are all important preventatives to adultery. These boundary issues must especially be addressed when adultery has already happened, been confessed, and a path has been charted towards healing and restoration. Processing the trauma, deciding to forgive and rebuild or forgive and move on, learning to cope with terrible memories, starting to build goodwill, learning to talk about the affair properly, cleaning up the fallout, nourishing recommitment, and moving forward – none of this is easy but it is not impossible. Indeed, it only becomes possible with the grace of God, counsel, and great heaps of patience. Nonetheless, as God Himself is the model of the betrayed spouse Who forgives His unfaithful children, so it is possible for redemption to follow infidelity.

Completing Your Marriage Preparation

Over the course of these ten chapters, you have walked through a grand vision of Christian marriage, have invested your time in thinking deeply about marriage, and conversed at length with your partner so that you can lay a deep foundation for your marriage. I, along with those who have helped me fashion this marriage preparation manual, wish you all the blessings that God intends for Christian marriage and pray that He would strengthen you to push on to maturity in the coming years so that on the Last Day you may present yourselves before the Lord and be crowned indeed with glory and honor!

I leave you now with this beautiful quote from the great and holy pedagogue of Christian marriage, St. John Chrysostom,

"Use marriage appropriately, and you shall be the first in the Kingdom and enjoy every good thing."[7]

Discussion Questions

1 What do you understand to be the meaning of your wedding rings?

2 What are the greatest enemies of marriage today, in your opinion? What do you consider to be the top obstacles to the long-term survival of your own particular marriage?

3 What are the harms that flow from premarital cohabitation?

4 Who in your lives can you turn to for encouragement in your marriage, especially if your marriage is strained?

5 What are the harms that may flow from the idealization of 'fairy-tale' marriage?

6 What do you want others to say about your marriage after you have reposed?

7 How does the understanding of the eternality of Christian marriage in general impact your thoughts about your own marriage?

Appendix - The Orthodox Rite of Marriage

THE ORTHODOX RITE OF MARRIAGE

THE BETROTHAL SERVICE

PRIEST: Hast thou, N., a good, free, and unconstrained will and a firm intention to take unto thyself to wife this woman N., whom thou seest here before thee?

GROOM: I have.

PRIEST: Hast thou, N., a good, free, and unconstrained will and a firm intention to take unto thyself to husband this man N., whom thou seest here before thee?

BRIDE: I have.

The Priest takes up one of the candles, lights it and gives it to the Groom, making before him the sign of the Cross as he does so; and having done the same for the Bride, the service begins:

DEACON: Master, bless.

PRIEST: Blessed is our God, always, now and ever, and unto ages of ages.

CHOIR: Amen.

During the Paschal season, the Paschal troparion is here sung thrice:
Christ is risen from the dead trampling down death by death and upon those in the tombs bestowing life.

THE LITANY of PEACE

DEACON: In peace, let us pray to the Lord.

CHOIR: Lord, have mercy.

DEACON: For the peace from above and the salvation of our souls, let us pray to the Lord.

CHOIR: Lord, have mercy.

DEACON: For the peace of the whole world, the good estate of the holy churches of God and the union of all men, let us pray to the Lord.

CHOIR: Lord, have mercy.

DEACON: For this holy house, and for those who with faith, reverence, and fear of God enter therein, let us pray to the Lord.

CHOIR: Lord, have mercy.

DEACON: For our Metropolitan N., the honorable presbytery, the diaconate in Christ, all the clergy and the people, let us pray to the Lord.

CHOIR: Lord, have mercy.

DEACON: For the servant of God, N., and for the handmaid of God, N, who now plight each other their troth, and for their salvation, let us pray to the Lord.

CHOIR: Lord, have mercy.

DEACON: That they may be granted children for the continuation of the race, and all their petitions which are unto salvation, let us pray to the Lord.

CHOIR: Lord, have mercy.

DEACON: That he will send down upon them perfect, and peaceful love, and his help, let us pray to the Lord.

CHOIR: Lord, have mercy.

DEACON: That he will preserve them in oneness of mind, and in steadfastness of faith, let us pray to the Lord.

CHOIR: Lord, have mercy.

DEACON: That he will bless them with a blameless life, let us pray to the Lord.

CHOIR: Lord, have mercy.

DEACON: That the Lord our God will grant unto them an honorable marriage, and a bed undefiled, let us pray to the Lord.

CHOIR: Lord, have mercy.

DEACON: For our deliverance from all tribulation, wrath, danger, and necessity, let us pray to the Lord.

CHOIR: Lord, have mercy.

DEACON: Help us; save us; have mercy on us; and keep us, O God, by thy grace.

CHOIR: Lord, have mercy.

DEACON: Calling to remembrance our all-holy, immaculate, most blessed and glorious Lady the Theotokos and ever-virgin Mary, with all the saints, let us commend ourselves and each other, and all our life unto Christ our God.

CHOIR: To thee, O Lord.

PRIEST: For unto thee are due all glory, honor, and worship to the Father and to the Son and to the Holy Spirit, now and ever, and unto ages of ages.

CHOIR: Amen.

DEACON: Let us pray to the Lord.

CHOIR: Lord, have mercy.

PRIEST: O eternal God, who hast brought into unity those who were sundered, and hast ordained for them an indissoluble bond of love; who didst bless Isaac and Rebecca, and didst make them heirs of thy promise: Bless also these thy servants, N., and N., guiding them unto every good work. For thou art a merciful God, who lovest mankind, and unto thee we ascribe glory: to the Father and to the Son and to the Holy Spirit, now and ever, and unto ages of ages.

CHOIR: Amen.

PRIEST: Peace be to all.

CHOIR: And to thy spirit.

DEACON: Let us bow our heads unto the Lord.

CHOIR: To thee, O Lord.

PRIEST: O Lord our God, who hast espoused the Church as a pure Virgin from among the

Gentiles: Bless this Betrothal, and unite and preserve these thy servants in peace and oneness of mind. For unto thee are due all glory, honor and worship, to the Father and to the Son and to the Holy Spirit, now and ever, and unto ages of ages.

CHOIR: Amen.

Then the Priest takes the ring of the Bride, and blesses the Groom, making with it the sign of the Cross thrice, touching the heads of the Bride and the Groom with it each time, and saying:

PRIEST: The servant of God, N., is betrothed to the handmaid of God, N., in the Name of the Father and of the Son and of the Holy Spirit.

CHOIR: Amen.

The Priest then places the ring on the fourth finger of the right hand of the Groom. Then the Priest takes the ring of the Groom, and blesses the Bride and the Groom, making with it the sign of the Cross thrice, touching the heads of the Bride and the Groom with it each time; and saying:

PRIEST: The handmaid of God, N., is betrothed to the servant of God, N., in the Name of the Father and of the Son and of the Holy Spirit.

CHOIR: Amen.

The Priest places the ring on the fourth finger of the right hand of the Bride. The Priest says the following prayer and the bridal pair exchange the rings when the Priest says, do thou now bless this putting on of rings.

DEACON: Let us pray to the Lord.

CHOIR: Lord, have mercy.

PRIEST: O Lord our God, who didst accompany the servant of the patriarch Abraham into Mesopotamia, when he was sent to espouse a wife for his lord Isaac, and who, by means of drawing of the water, didst reveal to him that he should betroth Rebecca: Do thou, the same Lord, bless also the betrothal of these thy servants, N., and N., and confirm the word which they have spoken. Establish them in the holy union which is from thee. For thou, in the beginning, didst make them male and female, and by thee is the woman joined unto the man as a helpmeet and for the procreation of the human race. Wherefore, O Lord our God, who hast sent forth thy truth upon thine inheritance, and thy covenant unto thy servants our fathers, even thine elect, from generation to generation: Look thou upon thy servant, N., and upon thy handmaid, N., and establish their betrothal in faith and in oneness of mind, in truth and in love. For thou, O Lord, hast declared that a pledge should be given and confirmed in all things. By a ring power was given to Joseph in Egypt; by a ring Daniel was glorified in the land of Babylon; by a ring the uprightness of Tamar was revealed; by a ring our heavenly Father showed his bounty upon his Son, for he said: place a ring upon his right hand, and bring the fatted calf and kill it, and let us eat and make merry. By thine own right hand, O Lord, thou didst arm Moses in the Red Sea; by thy true word the heavens were established, and the foundations of the earth were made firm; and the right hands of thy servants also shall be blessed by thine almighty word and by thine

upraised arm. Therefore, O Master, and, O Lord our God, do thou now bless this putting-on of rings with thy heavenly benediction: and let thine Angel go before them all the days of their life: For thou art he who blesseth and sanctifieth all things, and unto thee do we ascribe glory to the Father and to the Son and to the Holy Spirit, now and ever, and unto ages of ages.

CHOIR: Amen.

THE SERVICE of CROWNING

The Groom and Bride are led by the Priest to the analogion while the following psalm verses (Psalm 127) and refrain are being sung:

PRIEST: Blessed are all they that fear the Lord: and walk in his ways.

CHOIR: Glory to thee, our God; glory to thee.

PRIEST: Thou shalt eat of the fruit of thy labors: O blessed art thou, and happy shalt thou be.

CHOIR: Glory to thee, our God; glory to thee.

PRIEST: Thy wife shall be as a fruitful vine upon the walls of thy house: Thy children like a newly-planted olive-orchard round about thy table.

CHOIR: Glory to thee, our God; glory to thee.

PRIEST: Lo, thus shall the man be blessed that feareth the Lord: The Lord in Zion shall so bless thee, that thou shalt see the good things of Jerusalem all the days of thy life.

CHOIR: Glory to thee, our God; glory to thee.

PRIEST: Yea, that thou shalt see thy children's children, and peace upon Israel.

CHOIR: Glory to thee, our God; glory to thee.

DEACON: Bless, master.

PRIEST: Blessed is the kingdom of the Father and of the Son and of the Holy Spirit, now and ever, and unto ages of ages.

CHOIR: Amen.

During the Paschal season, the Paschal troparion is here sung thrice:

Christ is risen from the dead trampling down death by death and upon those in the tombs bestowing life.

THE LITANY of PEACE

DEACON: In peace, let us pray to the Lord.

CHOIR: Lord, have mercy.

DEACON: For the peace from above and the salvation of our souls, let us pray to the Lord.

CHOIR: Lord, have mercy.

DEACON: For the peace of the whole world, the good estate of the holy churches of God and the union of all men, let us pray to the Lord.

CHOIR: Lord, have mercy.

DEACON: For this holy house, and for those who with faith, reverence, and fear of God enter therein, let us pray to the Lord.

CHOIR: Lord, have mercy.

DEACON: For our Metropolitan N., the honorable presbytery, the diaconate in Christ, all the clergy and the people, let us pray to the Lord.

CHOIR: Lord, have mercy.

DEACON: For the servants of God, N., and N., who are now being united to each other in the community of marriage, and for their salvation, let us pray to the Lord.

CHOIR: Lord, have mercy.

DEACON: That he will bless this marriage, as he blessed that in Cana of Galilee, let us pray to the Lord.

CHOIR: Lord, have mercy.

DEACON: That he will give them chastity, and of the fruit of the womb as is expedient for them, let us pray to the Lord.

CHOIR: Lord, have mercy.

DEACON: That he will make them glad with the sight of sons and daughters, let us pray to the Lord.

CHOIR: Lord, have mercy.

DEACON: That he will grant them enjoyment of the blessing of children, and a blameless life, let us pray to the Lord.

CHOIR:　　Lord, have mercy.

DEACON:　That he will grant to them and to us, all our petitions which are unto salvation, let us pray to the Lord.

CHOIR:　　Lord, have mercy.

DEACON:　That he will deliver them and us from all tribulation, wrath, danger, and necessity, let us pray to the Lord.

CHOIR:　　Lord, have mercy.

DEACON:　Help us; save us; have mercy on us; and keep us, O God, by thy grace.

CHOIR:　　Lord, have mercy.

DEACON:　Calling to remembrance our all-holy, immaculate, most blessed and glorious Lady the Theotokos and ever-virgin Mary, with all the saints, let us commend ourselves and each other, and all our life unto Christ our God.

CHOIR:　　To thee, O Lord.

PRIEST:　　For unto thee are due all glory, honor, and worship to the Father and to the Son and to the Holy Spirit, now and ever, and unto ages of ages.

CHOIR:　　Amen.

FIRST PRAYER

DEACON:　Let us pray to the Lord.

CHOIR:　　Lord, have mercy.

PRIEST:　　O God most pure, fashioner of every creature, who didst transform the rib of our forefather Adam into a wife, because of thy love towards mankind, and didst bless them and say to them: Be fruitful and multiply, and fill the earth and subdue it; who didst make of the two one flesh: Therefore a man leaves his father and his mother and cleaves to his wife, and the two shall become one flesh, and what God hath joined together, let no man put asunder. Thou didst bless thy servant Abraham, and opening the womb of Sarah didst make him to be the father of many nations. Thou didst give Isaac to Rebecca, and didst bless her in childbearing. Thou didst join Jacob unto Rachel, and from them didst bring forth the twelve patriarchs. Thou didst unite Joseph and Asenath, giving to them Ephraim and Manasseh as the fruit of their procreation. Thou didst accept Zachariah and Elizabeth, and didst make their offspring to be the Forerunner. From the root of Jesse according to the flesh, Thou didst bud forth the ever-virgin one, and wast incarnate of her for the redemption of the human race. Through thine unutterable gift and manifold goodness, Thou didst come to Cana of Galilee, and didst bless the marriage there, to make manifest that it is thy will that there should be lawful marriage and procreation. Do thou,

the same all-holy Master, accept the prayers of us, thy servants. As thou wast present there, be thou also present here, with thine invisible protection. Bless this marriage, and grant to these thy servants, N., and N., a peaceful life, length of days, chastity, mutual love in the bond of peace, long-lived offspring, gratitude from their children, a crown of glory that does not fade away. Graciously grant that they may see their children's children. Preserve their bed un-assailed, and give them of the dew of heaven from on high, and of the fatness of the earth. Fill their houses with wheat, wine and oil and with every good thing, so that they may give in turn to those in need; and grant also to those here present with them all their petitions which are for their salvation. For thou art the God of mercies, and of bounties, and of love towards mankind, and unto Thee we ascribe glory: to the Father and to the Son and to the Holy Spirit, now and ever, and unto ages and ages.

CHOIR: Amen.

SECOND PRAYER

When the Priest says Bless them, O Lord our God, *he blesses the Groom and Bride with the hand Cross.*

DEACON: Let us pray to the Lord.

CHOIR: Lord, have mercy.

PRIEST: Blessed art thou, O Lord our God, the Priest of mystical and pure marriage, and the Ordainer of the law of the marriage of the body, the Preserver of immortality, and the Provider of good things; do thou, the same Master, who in the beginning didst make man and set him to be king over thy creation, and didst say: It is not good for man to be alone on the earth; let us make a helpmeet for him; Taking one of his ribs, thou and didst fashion Woman, which when Adam beheld, he said: This is now bone of my bone, and flesh of my flesh; she shall be called Woman; for this cause shall a man leave father and mother, and shall cleave unto his wife, and the two shall be one flesh; and those whom God hath joined together, let no man put asunder. Do thou now also, O Master, our Lord and our God, send down thy heavenly grace upon these thy servants, N., and N.; and grant that this thy handmaid may, in all things, be subject unto her husband; and that this thy servant may be the head of his wife, that they may live according to thy will.

PRIEST: Bless them, O Lord our God, as thou didst bless Abraham and Sarah:

CHOIR: Amen.

PRIEST: Bless them, O Lord our God, as thou didst bless Isaac and Rebecca:

CHOIR: Amen.

PRIEST: Bless them, O Lord our God, as thou didst bless Jacob and all the patriarchs.

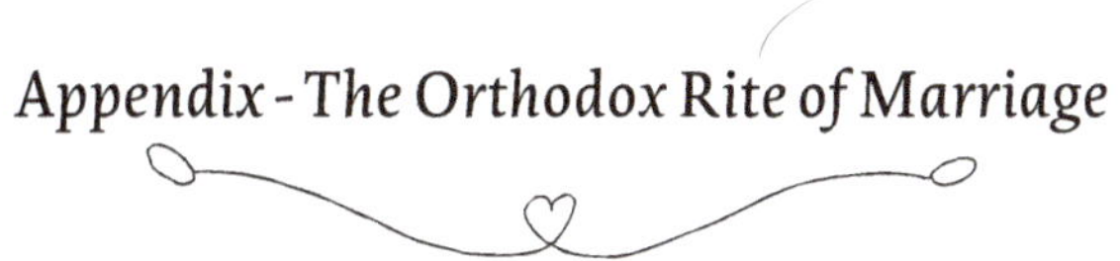

CHOIR: Amen.

PRIEST: Bless them, O Lord our God, as thou didst bless Joseph and Asenath.

CHOIR: Amen.

PRIEST: Bless them, O Lord our God, as thou didst bless Moses and Zipporah.

CHOIR: Amen.

PRIEST: Bless them, O Lord our God, as thou didst bless Joachim and Anna:

CHOIR: Amen.

PRIEST: Bless them, O Lord our God, as thou didst bless Zacharias and Elizabeth:

CHOIR: Amen.

Preserve them, O Lord our God, as thou didst preserve Noah in the Ark: Preserve them, O Lord our God, as thou didst preserve Jonah in the belly of the whale. Preserve them, O Lord our God, as thou didst preserve the three Holy Children from the fire, sending down upon them dew from heaven; and let that gladness come upon them which the blessed Helena had when she found the precious Cross. Remember them, O Lord our God, as thou didst remember Enoch, Shem and Elijah. Remember them, O Lord our God, as thou didst remember thy Forty Holy Martyrs, sending down upon them crowns from heaven: Remember them, O Lord our God, and the parents who have nurtured them, for the prayers of parents make firm the foundations of houses. Remember, O Lord our God, thy servants the attendants of the bridal pair, who share in this joy; remember, O Lord our God thy servant, N. , thy handmaid, N. , and bless them. Grant them of the fruit of their bodies fair children, and concord of soul and body; exalt them like the cedars of Lebanon, like a luxuriant vine. Give them offspring in number like full ears of grain; so that, having sufficiency in all things, they may abound in every work that is good and acceptable unto thee. And let them behold their children's children round about their table, like a newly-planted olive orchard, that, obtaining favor in thy sight, they may shine like the stars of heaven, in thee, our Lord and God: for unto thee are due all glory, honor, and worship together with thine unoriginate Father and thy life-giving Spirit, now and ever, and unto ages of ages..

CHOIR: Amen.

THIRD PRAYER

DEACON: Let us pray to the Lord.

CHOIR: Lord, have mercy.

PRIEST: O holy God, who didst create man out of the dust and didst fashion his wife and join her unto him as a helpmeet, for it seemed good to thy majesty that man should not be alone upon the earth: Do thou, the same Lord, extend thy hand from thy holy dwelling-place, and join

this thy servant, N., and this thy handmaid, N., for by thee is the husband united unto the wife. Unite them in one mind and wed them in one flesh granting them the fruit of the body and procreation of fair children. For thine is the majesty, and thine is the kingdom, and the power, and the glory of the Father and of the Son and of the Holy Spirit, now and ever, and unto ages of ages.

CHOIR: Amen.

THE CROWNING

The Priest takes up one of the wedding crowns and makes with it the sign of the Cross thrice over the heads of the Groom and the Bride, and touches the heads of the Groom and the Bride each time, saying:

PRIEST: The servant of God, N., is crowned unto the handmaid of God N., in the name of the Father and of the Son and of the Holy Spirit.

CHOIR: Amen.

The Priest places the Groom's crown upon his head and takes up the other crown and makes with it the sign of the Cross, thrice, over the heads of the Groom and the Bride, and touches the heads of the Groom and the Bride with it each time, saying:

PRIEST: The handmaid of God, N., is crowned unto the servant of God, N., in the name of the Father and of the Son and of the Holy Spirit.

CHOIR: Amen.

The Priest takes the Groom's crown in his right hand, and the Bride's crown in his left, and exchanges them thrice, chanting in tone seven:

PRIEST: O Lord our God, crown them with glory and with honor. *(thrice)*

THE EPISTLE

DEACON: Let us attend.

READER: Thou hast set upon their heads crowns of precious stones; they asked life of thee, and thou gavest it them.

(Verse): For thou wilt give them thy blessing forever and ever: thou wilt make them to rejoice with gladness through thy presence. (Psalm 2:3-4, 6)

DEACON: Wisdom.

READER: Lesson from the epistle of the holy Apostle Paul to the Ephesians.

DEACON: Let us attend.

READER: *(Eph. 5:20-33)* Brethren: Give thanks always for all things unto God and the Father, in the name of our Lord Jesus Christ; submitting yourselves one to another in the fear of God. Wives, submit yourselves unto your own husbands, as unto the Lord. For the husband is the head of the wife, even as Christ is the head of the Church: and he is the Savior of the body. Therefore as the Church is subject unto Christ, so let the wives be to their own husbands in everything. Husbands, love your wives, even as Christ also loved the Church, and gave himself for it; that he might sanctify and cleanse it with the washing of water by the word, that he might present it to himself a glorious Church, not having spot, or wrinkle, or any such thing; but that it should be holy and without blemish. So ought men to love their wives as their own bodies. He that loveth his wife loveth himself. For no man ever yet hated his own flesh; but nourisheth and cherisheth it, even as the Lord the Church: for we are members of his body, of his flesh, and of his bones. For this cause shall a man leave his father and mother, and shall be joined unto his wife, and they two shall be one flesh. This is a great mystery: but I speak concerning Christ and the Church. Nevertheless let everyone of you in particular so love his wife even as himself; and the wife see that she reverence her husband.

PRIEST: Peace be to thee that readest.

READER: And to thy spirit.

THE GOSPEL

CHOIR: Alleluia, alleluia, alleluia.

READER: Thou, O Lord, shalt protect us and preserve us from this generation forever. (Psalm 11:7).

CHOIR: Alleluia, alleluia, alleluia.

DEACON: Wisdom. Stand upright. Let us hear the holy gospel.

PRIEST: Peace be to all.

CHOIR: And to thy spirit.

PRIEST: Reading from the holy gospel according to Saint John the Theologian.

CHOIR: Glory to thee, O Lord. Glory to thee.

DEACON: Let us attend.

PRIEST: *(Jn 2:1-11)* In those days, there was a marriage in Cana of Galilee; and the mother of Jesus was there: and both Jesus was called, and his disciples to the marriage. And when they

wanted wine, the mother of Jesus saith unto him, They have no wine. Jesus saith unto her, Woman, what hast that to do with thee and me? Mine hour is not yet come. His mother saith unto the servants, "Whatsoever he saith unto you, do it." And there were set there six water pots of stone, after the manner of the purifying of the Jews, each holding twenty or thirty gallons. Jesus saith unto them, Fill the water pots with water. And they filled them up to the brim. And he saith unto them, Draw out now, and bear unto the governor of the feast. And they bare it. When the ruler of the feast had tasted the water that was made wine, and knew not whence it was: (but the servants which drew the water knew); the governor of the feast called the bridegroom, and saith unto him, Every man at the beginning doth set forth good wine; and when men have well drunk, then that which is worse: but thou hast kept the good wine until now. This beginning of miracles did Jesus in Cana of Galilee, and manifested forth his glory; and his disciples believed on him.

CHOIR: Glory to thee, O Lord. Glory to thee.

THE EKTENIA of FERVENT SUPPLICATION

DEACON: Let us all say with our whole soul and with our whole mind, let us say:

CHOIR: Lord, have mercy.

DEACON: O Lord almighty, the God of our fathers, we pray thee, hearken and have mercy.

CHOIR: Lord, have mercy.

DEACON: Have mercy on us, O God, according to thy great mercy, we pray thee, hearken and have mercy.

CHOIR: Lord, have mercy. Lord, have mercy. Lord, have mercy.

DEACON: Again we pray for mercy, life, peace, health, salvation and visitation for the servants of God N., and N., and their parents, and their attendants, and all here present.

CHOIR: Lord, have mercy. Lord, have mercy. Lord, have mercy.

PRIEST: For thou art a merciful God and lovest mankind, and unto thee we ascribe glory to the Father and to the Son and to the Holy Spirit, now and ever, and unto ages of ages.

CHOIR: Amen.

DEACON: Let us pray to the Lord.

CHOIR: Lord, have mercy.

PRIEST: O Lord our God, who in thy saving providence didst vouchsafe by thy presence in Cana of Galilee to declare marriage honorable: Do thou, the same Lord, now also maintain in peace and concord thy servants N., and N., whom thou hast been pleased to join together. Cause

their marriage to be honorable. Preserve their bed blameless, mercifully grant that they may live together in purity; even unto a ripe old age, walking in thy commandments with a pure heart: For thou art our God, the God of mercy and salvation, and unto Thee we ascribe glory together with thine unoriginate Father and thine all-holy and good and life-giving Spirit, now and ever, and unto ages of ages.

CHOIR: Amen.

THE LITANY BEFORE THE OUR FATHER

DEACON: Help us; save us; have mercy on us; and keep us, O God, by thy grace.

CHOIR: Lord, have mercy.

DEACON: That the whole day may be perfect, holy, peaceful and sinless, let us ask of the Lord.

CHOIR: Grant this, O Lord.

DEACON: An angel of peace, a faithful guide, a guardian of our souls and bodies, let us ask of the Lord.

CHOIR: Grant this, O Lord.

DEACON: Pardon and forgiveness of our sins and transgressions, let us ask of the Lord.

CHOIR: Grant this, O Lord.

DEACON: All things good and profitable for our souls and peace for the world, let us ask of the Lord.

CHOIR: Grant this, O Lord.

DEACON: That we may complete the remaining time of our life in peace and repentance, let us ask of the Lord.

CHOIR: Grant this, O Lord.

DEACON: A Christian ending to our life, painless, blameless, peaceful; and a good defense before the fearful judgment seat of Christ, let us ask.

CHOIR: Grant this, O Lord.

DEACON: Asking for the unity of the faith and the communion of the Holy Spirit, let us commend ourselves and each other and all our life unto Christ our God.

CHOIR: To thee, O Lord.

PRIEST: And vouchsafe, O Master, that with boldness and without condemnation we may

dare to call upon thee, the heavenly God, as Father, and to say:

THE OUR FATHER

Our Father, who art in heaven, hallowed be thy name; thy kingdom come; thy will be done on earth as it is in heaven. Give us this day our daily bread; and forgive us our trespasses as we forgive those who trespass against us. And lead us not into temptation, but deliver us from the evil one.

PRIEST: For thine is the kingdom and the power and the glory of the Father and of the Son and of the Holy Spirit, now and ever, and unto ages of ages.

CHOIR: Amen.

PRIEST: Peace be to all.

CHOIR: And to thy spirit.

DEACON: Let us bow our heads unto the Lord.

CHOIR: To thee, O Lord.

DEACON: Let us pray to the Lord.

CHOIR: Lord, have mercy.

THE COMMON CUP

Then the Priest says the following prayer of blessing of the Common Cup:

PRIEST: O God, who hast created all things by thy might, and hast made fast the round world, and adornest the crown of all things which thou hast made: Bless now, with thy spiritual blessing, this common cup, which thou dost give to those who are now united in the community of marriage: for blessed is thy name, and glorified is thy kingdom of the Father and of the Son and of the Holy Spirit, now and ever, and unto ages of ages.

CHOIR: Amen.

The Priest gives the newly-wedded pair to drink of the Cup, thrice each in turn, in token of their common life together, while the Choir sings (once) in tone one: I will take the cup of salvation and call upon the name of the Lord.

THE PROCESSION

In tone five: O Isaiah, dance thy joy: for a Virgin is with child and hath borne a son, Emmanuel, both God and man: and Orient is his name; whom magnifying we call the Virgin blessed.

In tone seven: Ye holy martyrs, who fought the good fight and have received your crowns: entreat ye the Lord that he will have mercy on our souls.

In tone seven: Glory to thee, O Christ our God: the Apostle's boast, the Martyrs joy, whose preaching was the consubstantial Trinity.

Then the Priest removes their crowns saying:

PRIEST: Be thou exalted, O Bridegroom, like unto Abraham; and be thou blessed, like unto Isaac; and do thou multiply like unto Jacob, walking in peace, and keeping the commandments of God in righteousness.

And thou, O Bride: Be thou exalted like unto Sarah; and exult thou like unto Rebecca; and do thou multiply like unto Rachel: and rejoice thou in thy husband, fulfilling the conditions of the law: for so is it well-pleasing unto God.

DEACON: Let us pray to the Lord.

CHOIR: Lord, have mercy.

PRIEST: O God, our God, who didst come to Cana of Galilee, and didst bless there the marriage feast: Bless, also, these thy servants, who through thy good providence are now united together in wedlock. Bless their goings out and their comings in: replenish their life with good things: receive their crowns into thy kingdom, preserving them spotless, blameless, and without reproach, unto ages of ages.

CHOIR: Amen.

PRIEST: Peace be to all.

CHOIR: And to thy spirit.

DEACON: Bow your heads unto the Lord.

CHOIR: To thee, O Lord.

PRIEST: May the Father and the Son and the Holy Spirit, the all-holy, consubstantial and life-giving Trinity, one Godhead, and one Kingdom, bless you; and grant unto you length of days, fair children, prosperity of life, and faith: and fill you with abundance of all earthly good things, and make you worthy to obtain the blessings of the promise: through the prayers of the holy

Theotokos, and of all the Saints.

CHOIR: Amen.

THE DISMISSAL

DEACON: Wisdom.

PRIEST: Most holy Theotokos, save us.

CHOIR: More honorable than the cherubim and more glorious beyond compare than the seraphim, thou who without corruption didst bear God the Word, and art truly Theotokos, we magnify thee.

PRIEST: Glory to thee, O Christ our God and our hope, glory to thee.

CHOIR: Glory to the Father and to the Son and to the Holy Spirit, both now and ever, and unto ages of ages. Amen. Lord, have mercy. Lord, have mercy. Lord, have mercy. Master, bless.

PRIEST: May he who by his presence at the marriage feast in Cana of Galilee didst declare marriage to be an honorable estate, Christ our true God; through the prayers of his all-holy Mother; of the holy, glorious and all-laudable Apostles; of the holy, God-crowned Sovereigns and Saints Equal-to-the-Apostles Constantine and Helena: of the holy Great Martyr Procopios; and of all the Saints, have mercy upon you and save you: forasmuch as he is good, and loveth mankind.

PRIEST: Through the prayers of our holy master, Lord Jesus Christ our God, have mercy upon us.

CHOIR: Amen.

DEACON: Grant, O Lord, a peaceful life, health, salvation and furtherance in all good things to thy servants N. and N., and preserve them for many years!

As the Choir sings the Many Years, the Priest blesses the couple with the hand Cross and then offers it to be reverenced by the Groom and Bride. The Groom and Bride kiss each other, go to their parents for a blessing, and then exit the church temple.

During the Paschal season, Through the prayers . . . *is not said but rather, the Paschal troparion is intoned once:*

PRIEST: Christ is risen from the dead trampling down death by death and upon those in the tombs . . .

CHOIR: . . .bestowing life.